MONEY ON MEANING

WHY WE DO WHAT WE DO

FOR LEADERS AT WORK

SURESH VERGHIS

INDIA • SINGAPORE • MALAYSIA

In loving memory of Acha who led a life of meaningful
leadership.

‘We shall meet on that beautiful shore’

Contents

Foreword

An excellent and challenging presentation! It has a personal touch as the young entrepreneur, busy with the training programmes for company employees and executives with a vision, unfolds his own personal experience on the rugged road to the 'Hall-of-Fame', with courage and determination guided by a personal vision. Nothing can be achieved without effort and determination in this world which is highly competitive.

Maintaining the secular nature of the book, he gives the reader an assurance that the 'universe' or the True Light, which enlightens everyone coming into this world, will come to one's help in times of uncertainty and indecision. The true light will guide you aright if you stick to your personal vision with integrity and tenacity.

He, in fact, draws the attention of the readers to an even worse situation as the whole world was facing and reeling under the Covid-19 pandemic. No one can predict what the new normal would be so one has to be more vigilant and ready for any change that might evolve out of the present chaotic situation.

I am extremely happy to note that the author, Suresh Verghis, has had a very encouraging experience in his journey in the Human Resources field. Having been brought to the attention of the prestigious George Washington University of Peace, USA, his hard-labour and research in the leadership realm for a number of years, facilitating and development for leaders at all levels, after proper scrutiny and testing, decided to award him the Degree of Doctor of Philosophy (Honoris causa). Honest and tireless labour will never be lost! So, I congratulate Dr. Suresh Mathew Verghis for this prestigious recognition he has earned through his hard labour and determination with a personal vision. The road may be rugged until one reaches the Hall of Fame!

Besides dealing with and drawing the attention of the readers to cardinal virtues and principles, the author intersperses his book with challenging and thought-provoking quotations from eminent and renowned persons who have contributed immense and exemplary services to the human society. For example, in Chapter 8 on Belonging, he introduces the following quotation from Dr. Martin Luther King (Jr.), the great Civil Rights Freedom Fighter of the 20th century in U.S.A:

"An individual has not started living until he can rise above the narrow confines of individualistic concerns to the broader concerns of all humanity."

Also, in Chapter 3, from Mahatma Gandhi, the Father of our Nation:

"Keep your thoughts positive, because your thoughts become your words; Keep your words positive, because your words become your behaviour; Keep your behaviour positive, because your behaviour becomes your habits. Keep your habits positive, because your habits become your values; Keep your values positive, because your values become your destiny."

These statements, taken seriously, impact visions by which one's life is glorified. Furthermore, in all chapters, he describes facets of leadership that the men and women of repute he quotes, displayed and rose to the pinnacle of glory overcoming many hazards in their lives, through their vision and determination, reminding the readers that, "Lives of great men, all remind us, we can make our lives sublime…" ("A Psalm of Life" by Henry Wadsworth Longfellow).

I wish the author Dr. Suresh Mathew Verghis, God's blessings and great success in his service to the society at large through his labour and research in the field of Leadership Development; and the readers, the guidance of the Eternal True Light, in their journey and sincere services on the rugged road, to 'The Hall of Fame.'

Rev. Dr. Jacob Verghis (late)

Formerly Principal of the Kerala United Theological Seminary and

President of the Board of Theological Studies of The Senate of Serampore College

Thiruvananthapuram

October 2020

Prologue

This book is dedicated to my father – mentor, leader and role model - the late Rev. Dr. Jacob Verghis who went to be with the Lord on 1st October 2023. He was a theologian, scholar and administrator having served as Principal of the Kerala United Theological Seminary and President of the Board of Theological Studies of The Senate of Serampore College. Dad was a lifelong learner and inculcated such values in us from a very early age. This record of work experiences has much to do with his guidance and vision.

"Lives of great men all remind us, we can make our lives sublime" is a line from H.W. Longfellow that I vividly remember my father quoting often during my early childhood days. This poem emphasizes the importance of living a meaningful, purposeful life. The line suggests that by looking at the lives of great individuals, we are inspired to achieve greatness in our own lives, to strive for something higher and more noble—making our lives "sublime." The poem also encourages readers not to dwell on the past or be overly concerned with the future, but rather to act in the present, make the most of every moment, and leave a positive impact on the world. Longfellow's message is one of optimism, resilience, and the belief that everyone has the potential to live a life that is both significant and inspirational.

This book is a leader's guide and companion to becoming more equipped and prepared for forays ahead in the world of work. Welcome to the leader's journey of self development. You have chosen well to invest in yourself. After all, who is more interested in our own development other than we ourselves.

This is a handy self-help book for professionals at all levels of leadership and those who aspire to be better leaders at the workplace. The book carries the reader through a set of selected facets of leadership right from formulating a personal vision, to nurturing your networking, aligning personal values, building leader behaviours, cultivating executive presence, learning the art of listening to connect without judgement, coaching for success, belonging in a diverse world, influencing with integrity, to having the courage for continuous development and significant areas of leadership in between.

Why do people work? Life and career are about money and meaning. Money is important. But many do not seek just money – they are constantly in need of connecting with their desires to do something that has meaning and is significant. A major part of a leader's role is to enable that meaning – for themselves and those they lead - to remind people why we do what we do, and why that matters.

An article written by Shawn Achor and others, was published in the Harvard Business Review on November 6, 2018, that highlights a significant finding from a survey of over 2,000 professionals across various industries: 'more than 9 out of 10 employees are willing to trade a portion of their lifetime earnings for the opportunity to do more meaningful work'. This suggests that for many, the value of meaningful work can outweigh financial compensation.

There were several motivations to write this book. Firstly, I turned 50 in the year of the pandemic. Turning 50 was a big deal. On my birthday, my life until then was played out in many memorable scenes cast in video messages that friends and family had sent in, in response to the secret requests from my wife, Annie and our daughter Neha. They colluded and collated these videos into one big production to give me a huge "50th" surprise. Thanks to the brilliant idea to present me this video compilation of wishes and memories, my lot was enriched – and their encouragement and enthusiasm greatly inspired this book.

Another great motivation to write this book is my ongoing exchange with the wide range of learners, leaders and coaches in my programs.

The objectives of this journey are multifold. They are - to engage, reflect and stimulate thinking – to understand the transactional and transformative thinking processes. Can we have balance between the two? How does this thinking serve the task on hand versus the relationship we need to maintain with each other. In other words, how do you balance task and relationship in any transaction?

How can one resolve to take action for transformation? Reading every chapter in this book calls for thinking and action. It would serve well to ask oneself, what is one takeaway from this chapter? What am I taking away to do, change or just think? A thinking action perhaps a good start to transformative thinking. Or a thought that brings in hope. Such thinking is intended to refresh, revive and reinforce action on various fronts at any time. This will certainly work immensely towards to one's personal development and hopefully evokes rich thinking.

I have provided some polls, open questions, summary points and calls to action that one can choose to follow through as a benefit from this reading experience. At the end of every chapter, you might take away something to do. This book contains experiences and learning that might stimulate you to try something new, or reinforce what was known but seldom tried at work.

Here are some reading guidelines for best results: find a quiet space that gives you a suitable environment to read. Do not worry unduly about getting interrupted. Relax. Keep gadgets aside, muted and preferably face-down. You can read a page at a time or a chapter at a time. Pause and reflect on each area of thought. Be self-aware and mindful of your train of thoughts. Do not rush through reading. You can use the read for quiet contemplation or for serious learning and sharing. Be emotional with yourself and ask questions freely. Give yourself permission to let go and immerse in reflective thinking.

Do share your experiences using the contact information provided. If you have a question, or a suggestion, please send it to us. We appreciate your time and value your thoughts. We invite you to enjoy this journey with us.

Dr. Suresh Mathew Verghis

"Lives of great men all remind us

We can make our lives sublime,

And, departing, leave behind us

Footprints on the sands of time."

"A Psalm of Life" by Henry Wadsworth Longfellow

01

Vision

My mother opened her mouth and let out a silent scream.

Wandering out of the kitchen, she had looked towards our third-floor balcony, and spotted me climbing up the railings of the balcony. She froze!

For no reason in particular, my father, who was busy in his study, chose that moment to take a break. He saw my mother down the hallway, shaking like a leaf, rooted to the ground. Sensing something amiss, he hurried towards her and looked in the direction of her frozen gaze. I turned and looked behind me, seeing both my parents seemingly ready to play catch-me-if-you-can, giggled and climbed up the last two rungs of the railing.

In an instant, my father was beside me, and had grabbed me from behind - before I could fall off the balcony. If he hadn't taken those quick giant steps, this story might have been written differently.

I swallowed hard when my father told me about this incident years later. What if I had fallen off? What had made my mother leave the kitchen, or my father his study, at that exact moment that they did? I did not think much about this then, but I did recall the incident when I started thinking of my 'purpose' in more recent times. It contributed to the process of understanding myself and knowing myself – the process of self-discovery!

Let's begin by trying to understand self-discovery as a means of getting to a personal vision.

SELF-DISCOVERY

I look at myself in the mirror - not in elaborate analysis of my appearance, but in an attempt to think deeper and look beyond, in self-discovery. Why was I saved at the last minute? What is the purpose for my existence? Is there truly a reason for being, a reason for existence? I felt that there is probably a larger purpose in life that I need to discover for myself.

The clearer the purpose gets, the clearer the path towards that purpose becomes. A personal vision evolves - all the more necessary in times of uncertainty.

Life changed drastically for some, less for others, during the pandemic of 2020-22. We lost many souls too soon. Pandemics, wars and economic downturns sometimes happen without much warning. There is a spreading sense of trepidation everywhere. What would help us stay our course?

I am sure that the floodgates would open up if I were to ask everyone what they had 'discovered' about themselves while locked down and quarantined, living through the 'mother of all VUCA' situations: volatile – uncertain – complex - and ambiguous.

When I took a class on Change Management for a group of executives, we talked about VUCA situations - not knowing that the COVID-19 pandemic was about to change the world. None of us were around, a hundred years ago, when the last pandemic happened. The 1918 pandemic took three years to subside. At the time of writing, the deadly pandemic has given rise to a few variants and many lives have been lost, destinies changed forever. But such a situation is also ideal ground for self-discovery. It is an opportunity such as no other, to learn, to research and to reflect.

What have you discovered about yourself during this pandemic period and its aftermath? What has your family or your close friend, spouse, partner, or significant other discovered about you?

This is what some of my training participants had to say when I posed the question to them:

"I realized that I am not bad at cooking."

"I learnt how to survive alone."

"I realized I can write poems and illustrate my writing."

"I can survive with bare essentials."

"I discovered that I'm patient in the most negative times."

"Nothing is more important than family."

"I understood how much we take our parents for granted."

"I learned there is a fine balance, and too much of anything is bad."

We all realized that it hasn't been all bad - The pandemic brought new opportunities for many - new skills, new learnings and new ways of working. When I polled my session participants who like everyone else back in June 2020 were stuck at home under government-imposed lockdowns, many said their mobile devices kept them occupied with social media and entertainment, and an equal number said that they settled into household chores. Others chose reading and watching Netflix, or spending time with family members, and sleeping, in that order.

Hats off to all you who kept yourselves occupied with something – changed your perspective, innovated, or did nothing at all — Whatever you did was something out of the ordinary. You discovered more and more about yourself.

Looking at the scenario at the time of writing this book, it is a mixed bag out there - people who have lost jobs; people who are lucky to retain jobs though with reduced salaries; people who are not affected at all. Some companies have had to cut back on salary spends, reversing them later, while there are others handing out salary increases right in the middle of the pandemic, to boost employee morale. Some businesses thought that they were recession-proof but soon discovered they were wrong! When things got back to normal, some businesses may have vanished. And new ones have emerged. The much touted 'new normal' is already normal – aided by human ability to replace the past with the present. It is possibly still an evolving state.

In discovering ourselves, we spot trends and changes that are happening all around us all the time. Using the discoveries, we've made about ourselves, let us equip ourselves for what is coming up - What's 'in', what's hot, what's the future, what's no longer relevant... We need to equip ourselves with tools and techniques, skills and hacks that will help us become smarter in managing the here and now, the today and tomorrow, whilst continuing to dream - for dreams are what make us forge onwards in our visualization of the future. As we do so, the visibility of the world around us, and possibly, of the path forward, will get clearer. It is all within the purview of self-discovery.

YOUR LIFELINE

A good exercise of self-discovery leading to thinking of your personal vision is to plot your lifeline. A 'lifeline' is a graph of defining incidents in your life so far, plotted by year on a number-line.

Look at yourself in the mirror. Or take a picture of yourself. Reflect on what you observe. What are you seeing? What pops into your mind first when you see yourself? Allow your mind to wander into your life's experiences. Think about real examples your life's highs and lows, successes and failures, good times and bad, the formative events of your life and the people who played a role in them - recall vivid details of what really took place.

Try to remember specific incidents. Recall the faces of people, visualize the surroundings, and try to recollect your thoughts at that time. Observe how the mind gently nudges the memories into view, letting you relive each moment as you enter and exit those scenes.

You can refer Sample Worksheet 1 towards the end of this chapter and follow the instructions to construct your lifeline. As you connect those points of your lifeline from the time you were born up until now, observe the sloping highs and lows; step back often to look at your graph overall. Absorb the lifeline you have plotted. Reflect on your life so far when you answer these questions:

1. How did you feel about yourself at these high points?

2. How did you feel about yourself at the low points?

3. What influence did the people and events you included in your lifeline have on your life?

4. How do you think these events have influenced your career decisions?

Share your thoughts with a trusted friend if you can. What were your goals then? What were your unique or personal moments? What are you feeling at this point? Hear yourself speak the words. How do they sound? This is an opportunity for you to hear yourself talk about your life-line highs and lows, your top-of-the-mind feelings about them and how they have influenced your future goals. That is a great way for you to get to know yourself, discover deep truths and strengthen your intentions.

PERSONAL EFFECTIVENESS

Having a personal vision boosts personal effectiveness. A professional's personal effectiveness framework has at its very foundation, self-leadership. There are two elements in self-leadership: task and relationship. For self-leadership, one needs to understand more about oneself. When you understand yourself first, you begin to understand others better. Plotting your life-line highs and lows and understanding their meaning in your life is all about understanding oneself. When we understand ourselves better, we try to understand others and manage relationships with them. A step-by-step route to personal effectiveness is important, starting with identifying one's goals or vision.

Throughout the process of self-discovery and understanding oneself in order to understand and manage others, there is the common thread of 'communication'. How do you communicate with yourself? How do you communicate with others? How do you communicate at different levels? It is this framework that is used throughout the journey in this book; attempting to understand more about yourself and acquire the tools and techniques to become a better professional, a better manager and a better leader.

In thinking about life's purpose or a personal vision, there are likely to be obstacles and roadblocks in life and one's career journey. The higher the odds, the more challenging it is to take the positive view of adverse situations and see the glass 'half-full', rather than 'half-empty'. If the intention is to move forward and face these challenges, we have little choice but to accept these problems as challenges. The path to any goal or vision will be fraught with challenges that will make us stronger if we choose to face them with tenacity.

Tenacious people are able to act upon those challenges and convert them to opportunities that will work for them. However, people are sometimes afraid of trying new things. The odds may have been too many or they may have been around for too long. A young friend talked about accidentally trying something new, and then realizing: 'Wow, I can do this too'. There is always a first time, and the first time could be awkward. But after that first attempt, the experience is no longer alien. So, all things considered, try anyway: you might win - or you might lose. These are the only two possibilities. We intend to win always, we do everything to guarantee success, take strenuous efforts and prepare relentlessly with a winning mindset. We may still win or lose, but if we lose all is not lost because we can learn from failure. Therefore, the mantra of overcoming the fear of trying is to "try anyway - win or lose, you certainly learn". This shift in thinking helps us in establishing a fearless mindset over time while we work on achieving our goals towards our vision.

You will become great professionals, great managers, and great leaders. You will lead yourselves, your teams and your businesses. Wherever you are, you need to be a leader to lead yourself and lead in the situations you encounter.

The key to unlocking learning is 'to be shameless and fearless to learn', never being afraid to ask 'how' and 'why'; never being afraid to ask a question to know and understand more about what you are curious about or make a comment or a statement that expresses your views or suggestions, as long as you stay relevant to the topic, time, place and accepted norms. People sometimes fear embarrassment and ridicule when they express ignorance. One's earliest experiences of ridicule and loss of self-esteem could usually come from formative school years where interactions with certain teachers or seniors could have resulted in uncharitable or undesirable behaviours for merely asking questions for clarification or making statements which may have been judged as plain 'stupid'. Personally, I have been petrified of this myself. The fear always is: 'what if I asked a question and it is called out as 'stupid'?' What if a comment or answer invited ridicule? What if everyone laughed and poked fun at me? Rejection is awkward and uncomfortable. I thought I would never ask questions again. I thought I would never express a point of view. But in time, fortunately, that changed for me. It needed to change, because of my need to establish a path forward was far too compelling for me to bother about passing ridicule.

While discussing these experiences, a senior of mine shared an incident from his 9th-grade in school. He was trying to make the point about how an innocent quip from him invited instant ridicule from the teacher, but also how he learnt to deal with it years later. The teacher had asked the class of 14-year-olds where they would like to go for that year's school picnic. My friend, in all his innocent enthusiasm, a certain geography class still fresh in his mind, jumped up and yelled joyfully: 'Let's go to the Grand Canyon!' The teacher spontaneously scorned him, berating the poor child for the 'impractical and silly' suggestion, and the whole class burst out laughing. My friend slowly sat down, his face turning pale. 'I remember I felt stupid back then,' he said many years later. Navigating a world of hardship and buoyed by some successes along the way, he trained himself to be 'shameless and fearless to learn', going on to become a successful Coach helping people become super-achievers by overcoming their own self-limiting beliefs, low self-esteem and ridicule. The story isn't over. A classmate who sat on the same bench next to him that day, slipped his hand into my friend's hand and squeezed it, knowing nothing about the future, but saying with simple compassion: 'Don't feel sad, I will take you to the Grand Canyon one day.' Ten years later, my friend got a call from his classmate. He, who had been to the US for higher studies, invited my friend over for a visit. They were reunited at the Grand Canyon.

You might face ridicule and humiliation. But remember, you alone are the author of your life. Be sure to edit, and perfect your script. While doing so, you are learning more about yourself and your opportunities. You are strengthening yourself to face a world of failure and success. So, try anyway. Personal effectiveness is an outcome of understanding oneself, managing oneself as well as understanding others and managing others.

FORMULATING YOUR PERSONAL VISION

With what we know so far in self-discovery and personal effectiveness, how could we create a Personal Vision? Do you have a Personal Vision formulated yet? If you do not, you are not alone. Few can define their long-term goals early in life, design their education path accordingly and chart out a near-perfect course for a career. Many, like me, discover our careers by luck and opportunity, and not necessarily by design. Whichever category you belong to, always remember that you are one among tens of thousands in the same boat. Knowing that, let's ask ourselves what we can do to bring more purpose, meaning and fulfilment into life. The answer is to work on a Personal Vision.

A Personal Vision attracts commitment. It is energizing. It creates meaning in one's life. It establishes a standard of excellence. It bridges the present and the future. It transcends the status quo. It is an inspiring statement that depicts your life in the future – a beautiful way to express your personal vision.

To pursue building a vision, think about your life in the future. Allow a visual scene to develop in your mind. Take your time with formulating this visual – a scene that you can imagine yourself in – imagine you have achieved that vision or goal. A depiction, or a painting takes time to form on canvas with slow and deliberate strokes. The images, form, style, words, or sentences used in your vision are unique to you. If you formulate your 'vision' into a vision statement, only remember that it is not created to win others' approbation. You are depicting your vision of your future, and this is only for yourself. It is an important visual or statement that makes sense only to you. It is therefore unique and exclusive. One does not seek others' approval on it. However, one might make adequate research and information gathering towards the achievement of the milestones.

My session participants or coachees sometimes say, "I have a vision, but I am not sure if I will achieve it. What if it is not achievable? What if it is challenging to achieve?" and so on. "Aim for the sun, and you might reach the stars," I might say. And probably the stars are what will help you achieve your goals ultimately. It is not up to us to judge the vision based on self-doubt and assumptions. Steven Covey, in his book, The Seven Habits of Highly Effective People, says in his 2nd Habit, "Begin with the end in mind." That is all we are doing. That is all we need to do. You need to have an end (goal) in mind. It is like using an application like Google Maps to guide you to your destination. What do you do first when you want to drive somewhere that is unfamiliar to you? You punch in the destination and the app then gives you a recommended route to reach your destination together with a couple of other options. You then choose the route. But unless you know where to go, how can you decide which route to take?

That reminds me of the Cat's words in Alice in Wonderland. "Would you tell me, please, which way I ought to go from here?" Alice asked the Cheshire cat. The Cat replied, "That depends a good deal on where you want to get to". "I don't much care, where--" said Alice. "Then it doesn't matter which way you go," said the Cat. "—so long as I get somewhere," Alice added as an explanation. "Oh, you are sure to do that," said the Cat, "if you only walk long enough."

Most people end up in Alice's situation without realizing it. They choose a path that seems to take care of the immediate needs, with not much of an idea where it will take them eventually. Not all are lucky enough to land up on a path that will take them to their ideal destination. But determining the general location of the destination will make sure you take steps that will reach you at least somewhere close.

Your Personal Vision Statement is for you to write, read, reflect and be happy about. It is important to you because it is your vision. It is your goal in life, your direction. It is what you are pursuing. It is what you establish as a target. When you have an idea of the overall direction, you end up doing many activities related to that direction and destination. That is why your vision statement is unique. People may choose the same destination, but different paths to reach it, depending on their circumstances.

Different paths. A few decades ago, the thinking was – "make a plan and stick to the plan". Not anymore. The Vision or goal can be fixed or changed anytime. However, it consists of a host of short-term plans that you intend will reach you to your ultimate goals. Many of us tend to think about the future of these plans with trepidation. The Vision Statement helps calm that feeling by providing a beacon light in the distance.

Some are not sure about, or not satisfied with their crafting of the statement. This is quite a natural feeling because our minds are conditioned to make everything we do seem perfect to others. But, as a reminder, this vision exercise is not for others' approval. It is about your own future as perceived in the here and now. One can change it as we travel along, as priorities and circumstances change, as experiences are gathered. If anyone had asked me in my late teens or early tweens, what my vision statement was, I would probably have said that I just would like to be the best in whatever I do or reach the highest levels in my field of work. I could not define it then as I can now. Experience helps.

"There's a mental or first creation, and a physical or second creation to all things, said Steven Covey while describing his 2nd habit. "The more you spend in meditation, the clearer and more detailed you can see your future goals."

It took a few years for my personal Vision Statement to evolve. This is what it says now, finetuned well into my mid-forties:

"To help leaders achieve sustained change in behaviours,

to elevate performance and personal success."

Did I start my life or career with my personal vision all defined and ready to go? Not at all. My overall desire for a particular type of career was formed early. I intended to work with people in a human resources function, helping them learn and perform. Twenty years in corporate human resources helped me do what I loved. But it wasn't enough to entirely satisfy my ikigai I guess. When I started my second career, I was already on my way towards an undefined vision, a desirable destination, nevertheless. Many of us start off in this manner. We might also take the help of role models to chart out several roadmaps to our destination.

Twenty-four years later, a process workshop by Dr. T. T. Srinath helped me crystallize my thoughts on the direction and come close to crafting my Vision Statement in a two-stage exercise. It was challenging initially. But the Vision Board exercise in stage one, helped me think about my personal vision and life goals and put down the visuals that formed in my mind, onto paper in the form of pictures. The task is to draw out on paper the mental picture of 'where I want to reach' as if 'I have already arrived' there. The drawings and words that represented this 'arrived-at-destination' scene, enlivened by colours, began to shape my vision, later formulated into words to form a sentence - that became the Personal Vision Statement. I was also greatly inspired by the training I received from Dr Judith E. Glaser, neuroscientist and writer. Her body of work and research is monumental and so is her book titled 'Conversational Intelligence: How Great Leaders Build Trust and Get Extraordinary Results'.

Once you have a draft vision statement, according to Dr. Srinath, you could proceed to find deeper meaning in that vision, by 'humanizing' it. Humanizing is done by taking the help of a group of friends of the vision owner, the protagonist; and making each word or element come alive by having a person in the group who connects with a specific element, express himself or herself as being that element. This is a high reflection exercise and a group of participants who offer to be part of the humanizing exercise, need to stay in connection all through the duration of the exercise until they have exhausted all their thoughts. The vision owner remains the protagonist in this exercise and chooses to 'connect' and expand deeper or let go off the live natural expressions of the cohort.

The sample worksheet 2 at the end of this chapter lists a few things to keep in mind when you put pen to paper to frame a Personal Vision Statement.

REFLECTION

Ask yourself:

Do I have a vision?

Can I see a clear path forward?

Is my personal vision easy to write?

Is my vison or goals impossible to achieve?

Am I trying to put down a vision so that it looks good to someone else?

Can I visualize a vision or my goals taking shape in my mind?

Do I already see my vision or goals taking shape?

SAMPLE WORKSHEET 1
LIFE-LINE EXERCISE

Take a plain sheet of paper or your notebook and a pen. Draw a horizontal line on the paper or notebook page, from left to right, in the middle of the sheet. Write down your milestone years starting from your year of birth or the first year you remember on the sheet from left to right, just below the horizontal line. Think about the high points in your life so far – achievements, positive events, successes, milestones achieved. What were those high points, and when did they happen?

Use red, green, or black markers to write, depending on the nature of the event: green for biological events, red for physical events and black for psychological events. You might need to do a few drafts before making the final record of the events on a worksheet in chronological order.

Place an 'X' above the year in which you had a high. You can vary the height of that 'X' depending on how high (or how significant) the high point was. For a phenomenal achievement, you might place the 'X' entirely above the other high points. It is your perception of something that you are proud of. In other words, your most important achievements that you are the proudest of would get the highest height. Similarly, think about the low points in your life so far and place an 'X' below the line at a depth depending on 'how low the low was'. Use the colour markers as described above.

SAMPLE WORKSHEET 2
PERSONAL VISION EXERCISE

Create your Vision Board step by step using the following guidelines:

1. Think about your personal goals and aspirations.

2. Prioritize your goals.

3. Write down these goals and ideas on your vision board.

4. Think about the difference you can make to yourself and your loved ones.

5. How do you visualize them happening and taking shape?

6. Imagine you have achieved your goals.

7. Visualise the picture of having attained your goals in your mind (Steven Covey said – "begin with the end in mind").

   What does it look like?

   What does it sound like?

   What does it feel like?

8. Put down that visualization physically on your vision board by drawing, pasting paper clippings and writing appropriate words.

9. Sort and arrange the images and words over and over until it looks like the vision is achieved.

10. Complete your Vision Board. Iterate it over the next few days.

11. Do not restrict yourself in terms of words, form or style.

12. Feel free to express yourself. This Vision Statement is for your eyes only.

SUMMARY

- Think about your 'purpose'. Start knowing yourself in a process of self-discovery.

- The clearer the purpose gets, the clearer the path towards that purpose becomes.

- There is no better time than 'now', to learn, to research, to reflect.

- Dreams are what make us forge onwards in our visualization of the future.

- An exercise in self-discovery is to plot your lifeline of defining incidents in your life so far.

- Know yourself, discover deep truths and strengthen your intentions.

- The personal effectiveness framework has at its very foundation, self-leadership.

- The two elements in self-leadership, task and relationship need to be in good balance.

- A step-by-step route to personal effectiveness starts with identifying one's goals or vision.

- Accept problems as challenges. Convert them to opportunities.

- Overcome the fear of trying. Try anyway; you may win, you may lose - but you learn.

- The key to unlocking your learning is 'to be shameless and fearless to learn'.

- Steven Covey said, "Begin with the end in mind."

CALL TO ACTION

Ponder over your life-line highs and lows and write or draw your personal vision in words and pictures that make sense to you.

The founder of analytical psychology, Carl Jung, once remarked, *"Your vision will become clear only when you can look into your own heart. Who looks outside, dreams; who looks inside, awakes."*

02

Networking

"You can have everything in life you want if you will just help enough other people get what they want."

– Zig Ziglar

"We do not have a role for you. You can go back to your hometown."

The words pierced my ears. I was 24 years old. I started my HR career just the previous year. The company's CEO had hired me as a trainee HR executive, and everything seemed great just as in any start-up. Everything seemed fine until a human resources boss armed with premium credentials joined the company. More of his ilk followed, apparently to build a 'better', 'more professional' team. As you can imagine, matters hitherto simple in essence and approach started getting more complex. Hierarchies were established. Jargon ruled. Endless meetings followed. Posturing, lobbying, and boardroom 'analysis-paralysis' events became the norm. Like all good things which come to an end, my romance with the HR function and the organization too had come to an end. A year earlier, I had been conferred the best employee award for successfully completing a massive recruitment and training drive single-handedly, deploying the first newly trained sales force teams at the various branch locations, outlets and divisions across the company, taking the start-up's headcount from 10 to 150 in 3 months. The President's words to me were: "None of this has ever been done before for such a business; think through and innovate." The Group Chairman, who had heard of my performance from the President, remarked: "how can a young man just out of college onto his first job have such farsightedness, ownership and dedication - something senior folks can learn from". It was great to hear those words of appreciation early in my career. Work was challenging and stimulating. I had proved myself at an early age; life was good.

But all the feelings of euphoria were short-lived as I awaited my fate in the HR Boss's office. It was an ominous, intimidating and loathsome situation. I had just moved to the big city where the company was headquartered, about a year earlier, leaving my hometown for good. Or so I thought. My mother was upset for days, realizing I had left home to 'seek my fortune', and would only visit occasionally. And here I was, a year later, at the mercy of the HR Boss who was telling me to go back home! I could not believe my ears. As I returned to my living quarters that evening, it dawned on me that returning to my hometown was not an option. That night, during my customary weekly phone call, my parents sensed trouble. They were supportive and encouraged me to search for another work opportunity and take help from whoever I could. I certainly needed to survive in this new city, manage my personal needs and be self-sufficient. There was undoubtedly an urgency, but it was not a desperate situation. My head was in the right place.

The next few days saw me furiously creating my biodata and printing sufficient copies of it, calling a few friends, asking for references, and zipping around on my motorbike, trying to meet as many people as possible for an interview. I wanted to land a new job in a month. I was not going to allow anyone, or any situation define my future. I consulted a few friends in the industry who stepped in to help. Most were those with whom I had a good working relationship or simply had a great rapport. I was always known for being available to help and support colleagues and associates. Many lent me an ear; some offered reassuring words; others tried to look up phone numbers to help. In an era where the computer, internet, mobile phone and LinkedIn were still two or three years away from existence, I began to scour classified ads in newspapers for job vacancies and walk the streets, meeting acquaintances and trying to get introductions to new people. My objective was to build my network rapidly and gain interviews for jobs – and, most of all – to try to remain in the big city of opportunities. The HR boss could go to hell. I was not going back home yet.

The strong resolve, legwork and sweat paid off. In precisely 30 days, I was lucky enough to land two successful job interviews, one with an upcoming software services company, ('software' still at a nascent stage), and the other, with a long-standing automotive ancillary parts manufacturing company – I chose the path less travelled by, and that has made all the difference. All of this was possible in an era of 'no tech' networking. If we consider good old traditional networking, there is a lot we can learn from being authentic and the merit in being ever willing to support others in their need. That is precisely how my networking helped my job pursuits, throughout my career.

BUILDING YOUR NETWORK

"The currency of real networking is not greed but generosity."
-- Keith Ferrazzi

Networking is about being ready to give first even before you think of receiving. To ascertain the quality of one's network, it is necessary to ascertain the readiness and effectiveness of our network to fulfil our needs from time to time. Recently, at a team bonding session for my executive MBA students, all of them with work experience ranging from 2 to 6 years, I asked them if they were active on a professional networking platform such as LinkedIn.

9% said that they did not have a LinkedIn profile.

10% of the group had created their login details for their profile and left it at that.

27% of the group said that their profile was 50% updated.

54% felt that their profile was fully updated at that time.

The poll analysis told me two things: First, we do not usually think about our careers and networking as long as everything is progressing well and there are no imminent threats to our jobs and careers. Second, a group of professionals, though a minority, still do not know or are not aware of the benefits of staying connected in this highly networked world.

To build a career, one needs to have an online professional profile on a platform such as LinkedIn®, where one can be searched for or discovered by a potential employer or network contact. The online presence through this medium is quite widespread and far-reaching. While this is not an endorsement for any professional media platform in particular, LinkedIn is the largest and probably the only platform at present to cover such a wide range of professional networking services and bring professionals together worldwide. That said, I also know of LinkedIn® members who make it their goal to rapidly add large numbers of contacts to their profile. While the number of network members may look phenomenal, the strength of the connection, whether 'acquaintance, ally or advocate', is something one needs to think about. Increase your network members as long as you follow LinkedIn's recommended guidelines for security and safe conduct.

Building your network is valuable to building your career. A professional presence in the world of work enhances your visibility and public awareness of your credentials. Even if you don't have a large personal network, you already have a platform such as LinkedIn the moment you have an online professional presence. Such a platform is also a resource for self-development as you will find articles, posts and blogs written by its members. However, nothing beats the possibility of face-to-face meetings in industry conferences or professional seminars where better associations can be developed.

The ultimate benefit of networking as we know, is to gain value for ourselves. However, it is when you give, you can expect to receive. There could be occasions when you need immediate support, and the tendency is to go all out trying to get what you want. This is perfectly alright in networking. When you approach someone in your network for help, do so with openness and transparency. While it is desirable to come across as being open about the support you need, be mindful of potential consequences for the person you approach, because you might be asking for something that that the person might find challenging to provide. Be mindful of the possibility that your request could leave your network member embarrassed as they might be unable to fulfil your request for some reason or might have to bend backwards to meet it. The request must always be proportionate to the strength of your relationship. Strong connections often do not mind the occasional request for support. However, perception of the strength of the relationship can vary between network connections.

FEED THEM WHEN YOU DON'T NEED THEM

This might be the key to checking on strength of relationships. You may have had the experience of someone who has not been in touch with you for a long time call you up and say quite unabashedly, 'Hey, can you do me a huge favour?' People can be consumed by their own needs at that point such that they come straight to the point without any preamble or pleasantries, like "How are you? It's been a long time. I'm sorry, I was not in touch...", and going on to gently build up to seeking the favour. Does the brusque approach leave you with an awkward feeling? Quite likely so.

What is the important lesson here? You need to build your network and nurture it even when you do not need it so when you really need to leverage your network, it is warm, ready and willing! Also, your perception of the strength of your relationship is better, though this should not be taken as a given. There is no harm making a request where you feel you have a credit of doing a favour.

Invest your time in people who can be your ambassadors. They might not be your ambassadors today, but they have the potential to be ambassadors later. You might have no use for somebody today, but you never know who can turn out to be an angel in disguise in the future. Hence do not discount anybody. Many early-career connections later turn into powerful allies. A decade or more into your career, you might realize that someone can help you with something and, but you really have not been in touch with them, and it's a little awkward now to ask them now for an important favour. It is ideal to minimize such situations and gently build up to revive your connections.

Nurture your network as you would a relationship. The more you give, the more you get. It is about giving without expecting anything in return. People who have given away resources in support without expecting anything in return have found their rewards much later in life. A connection here, a referral there, a testimonial for a colleague, a request to connect, are all opportunities to nurture your network. And when you have received these gifts, pay them forward. Such gestures nurture your career and network. You grow potential allies who might support you out in times of need. The more you are supportive the more people tend to like you. You can generally influence people who like you, and vice versa.

Who are your network connections? How well do you know them? How often do you keep in touch with them? In what forums do you interact with them? What sort of people are you in touch with? An exercise to classify your network and differentiate among them is given at the end of this chapter. It categorises your network into three: acquaintances, allies and advocates.

AQUAINTANCES IN YOUR NETWORK

An acquaintance is someone with whom you have a minimal level of interaction. You may know each other by name or recognize them in passing. You might meet occasionally. They might be people you may acknowledge on your routine path as they turn up in the same place around the same time every other day. You might just know each other as familiar faces or you may just wish them a good day, no more. There may be people in your phone book who are acquaintances from brief interactions. You know the services they do. Or you are probably just getting to know each other. They are people who you might not rely on for a large favour. Your knowledge of them or your relationship with them is not strong enough for you to ask them for support or even influence them. It is prudent not to assume that an acquaintance can be made into an ally quickly, unless there is an immediate need to support each other, and the relationship develops on a mutual basis. Relationships generally take time to develop. It takes a number of a variety of interactions for an acquaintance to become an ally. Hence is important never to rush into a relationship and force acquaintances to become allies, however much they are potentially useful to you. This can be off-putting, and one can jeopardise a potential relationship rather quickly, as people generally resent being pressured into relationships unless they see value in them. Acquaintances are however people who can potentially become allies, provided there is sufficient ground for a reciprocal relationship.

ALLIES IN YOUR NETWORK

Who are allies? Allies are those who know your talents and aspirations. They know your successes and can talk about them. Your degree of familiarity is high, and you find that they go out of their way to support you and even give you feedback. They care about your success. They might provide you with advice and you respect and accept such advice. They are knowledgeable about your expertise, your competence and your character. When somebody is convinced of your competence and character, the chances are that they will talk about you at available opportunities. They will make sure the right people hear about you. And you might do the same for them. You might have supported the ally such that the ally reciprocates seamlessly. You have a rather symbiotic relationship going. Your ally is someone with whom you can request a favour with respect and care and your ally does the same to you. You can be candid with each other if there is going to be a challenge in provided the support or help that is requested for. You know that a real ally will not mind that you have this challenge, and you can be open about it. This is possible when the degree of trust is high. Acquaintances and allies could be very different in many respects. The stress on our minds could be high because of our needs and in our over-enthusiasm, we mix them up and ask of one set what we should ideally be asking of the other. This can potentially strain the relationship. So, before making a request, think through carefully. In our eagerness to get a job done or obtain a favour, we might actually be tapping parts of our network which we are not ready to be allies yet. Remember, the request for support must always be proportionate to the strength of your relationship.

ADVOCATES IN YOUR NETWORK

Advocates are people who talk to others on your behalf. They are people who know you well. They believe in your abilities and skills. They are confident of your performance and your integrity. They are willing to put their good name on the line on your behalf. That is as strong as a reference or testimonial as you can get - when someone advocates for you, they are putting their name on the line for you. They vouch for your expertise, competence and character. They make sure that the right people hear about you. That means that they keep you in mind or connect an opportunity with your capability instantly, even if you are out of sight. They recall your name when asked for a reference. You trigger an instant recall when there is a request for an expertise you possess. Advocates are those who support your referral, and you might do the same for them. Unlike allies, you and your advocates may or may not have a reciprocal relationship of advocacy. This is alright as advocates are those who are recipients of your services, excellence or successes. They are impacted in one or more possible ways and have possibly experienced your capabilities at some point in time. This would generally be a small group of people, but their endorsements are quite powerful.

When you analyse your network thoroughly, and understand its components, you will also understand where you need to focus to build your network. To help you do this, further subdivide your acquaintances, allies and advocates into the following four categories: first look within the organization you work in, second, the profession you are qualified or certified in, or third, whether they belong to the same industry. You can also find out who your acquaintances, allies and advocates are, in your personal or family spheres, a fourth category.

THE NETWORK WITHIN YOUR ORGANISATION

Now let us take them one by one starting with the easiest one. How do we build the three levels of the network in an organization you are associated with? How can you grow your acquaintances, allies and advocates within the institution you work in currently or have worked in before? The organisation you work in is the best place to start networking simply because you spend most of your waking hours at work. It would do you good, not only to know the colleagues who work within tour team but also those who work in other teams, functions and verticals. It is a great opportunity to learn more about different functions of your organisation and be knowledgeable about key operations, projects, people and systems. To attract your network towards yourself, and nurture it, get familiar with your organization's vision, mission, values, strategic goals, norms, key customers, leaders, important trends, projects and initiatives. Make sure that you have an all-round view of your organization as well as complete familiarity with interesting organisational highlights, historical milestones and former leaders who have shaped the organisation over the years. This is useful, because people within the organisation love to talk to well-informed people. That surely does not mean being more inquisitive than one should, but having a healthy curiosity and deep interest in the organisation's progress is very useful. Keep your eyes open and ears to the ground. Generally, be in the know of what's happening. Make a list of your current acquaintances, allies and advocates at work.

Reflect on how to upgrade them from acquaintances to allies and allies to advocates.

THE NETWORK WITHIN YOUR PROFESSION

The next sub-segment is your profession. Who are the acquaintances, allies and advocates in your profession? Engineering in general is a profession. You might know other engineers, your course mates, classmates and peers in the college courses you have undertaken. You might still be in touch with them. These people share the same or similar professions but might not be in your organization. Networking with them has immense value. Know your specific professional associations - HR networks, Engineers Guild, management associations, consultants' network and so on. Read professional publications and blogs, know who the key players and leaders in your field are. Networking in your area of practice helps increase your expertise and extend your influence. It helps you know where opportunities exist and who might be able to help you gain further connections within the profession. Professional associations such as the International Coaching Federation have very well-run chapters all over the world. They exist to grow the profession and practice of coaching. Professional development is a top priority of most profession-based networks and associations. They help you connect with mentors within those professional fields who not only guide you on your professional development but also point you in directions suited to your interests and passion. They connect you with other professionals who can provide you career oriented advice and guidance. Many great career moves happen even in one time chance meetings with connections of connections. You get to be known over time within your profession, and that will help you with various milestones of your career.

THE NETWORK WITHIN YOUR INDUSTRY

List down your acquaintances, allies, and advocates from within your industry. Industry seminars and association meetings are a great way to connect with not just people from your profession but also from your industry. They may or not may not share your profession domain qualifications but are within the same environment that your organisation operates. When you meet such industry connections, you can discuss overall trends in the industry, changing technology, new leaders, emerging or declining organisations, and those that are either interesting start-ups or matured organisations. Many businesses have survived the 2020 pandemic or have perished. And many will emerge because a worldwide recession could result in a 'global reset' for business and economy. After the reset, a new normal may have emerged in certain pockets but in many cases, it is business as usual. People and businesses will continue to evolve. The changes will become more and more evident over time. There can be a lot of flux. We have to be prepared for change in such situations. We need to keep our eyes and ears open to the news and information that keep trickling in. Business news and information sites tell you a lot about what is happening in your profession and your industry. You will know which companies are growing or declining, what new products or services are trending, and the innovations being made. They may be virtual businesses or app-based businesses or traditional brick-and-mortar businesses. Many people tried to convert their existing services to online or virtual services and were trying to figure out how to innovate operating their existing businesses without the physical contact. There were many innovative new ways of doing business triggered by the pandemic and many of these have either survived or changed their business model altogether to suit a hybrid go-to-marker approach.

During the pandemic I was talking to my classmate, a renowned cardiologist, about the new ways of consultation for patients. I asked him, "Are you going to have your consultation room with a glass partition where you sit behind plexi glass and your patient out of contact with you completely? Does that work for you?" He said, "No, my specialisation needs more contact. There's going to be physical touch, but we're going to do some social distancing, use gloves, personal protective suit and all those things." Nobody knew then what the new normal would entail. Doctors especially did not know how they're going to consult given this particular situation. There was so much we did not know. But there was so much that people all over the world got used to. That is what we call the new normal. Many different trends have emerged as a result. All these and more are what you gain in knowledge from being in touch with your industry. It helps figure out proactive ways to change methods, approach, strategy, or simply prepare yourself for the next career phase or challenge.

THE NETWORK IN YOUR PERSONAL LIFE

Finally, we come to acquaintances, allies, and advocates in personal life. I'm sure whichever stage you are in your career, you will be able to identify many of them at each level. These connections in personal life could also become your professional advocates at some point in time. Personal life connections could range from relatives to friends, to school mates, classmates, college mates, friends or colleagues of parents and their connections or even a distant relative. However, people often discount personal connections as those who could support them professionally, either because they are so used to them over time that they can't fathom their support in a professional situation, or they have grown with the connection over the years that they have simply overlooked the possibility of support of a professional nature. They may have discounted their support and influence in their spheres of development. Those who connect with their personal connections seeking advice and guidance at different stages of their careers might find that they are able to nurture and grow their careers in ways that have benefitted them in the long run. The network in your personal life is possibly the strongest amongst allies and advocates since there is personal investment in personal connections.

SAMPLE WORKSHEETS

Draw three vertical columns on a sheet of paper. Write the three headings, Acquaintances, Allies and Advocates, one heading each column. Now draw 4 rows, horizontally and title each row as Organisation, Profession, Industry and Personal. Now write down the names of people who you consider as acquaintances in your organisation, allies in your organisation and advocates in your organisation. Use the definitions that were provided to understand who belongs to which category. Use the list as a starting point to build your circle of acquaintances, allies and advocates in each of the horizontal areas. Soon you will find that you have a large list of acquaintances, a smaller list of allies and a still smaller list of advocates in each row category: organisation, profession, industry and personal. This is a great start to know your network as it is and generate ideas on your next step.

TIP: The idea is not to have a large number of advocates but grow your acquaintances into allies.

TAKEAWAYS AND REFLECTION

1. Explore your online presence with LinkedIn or other professional platforms. Check your profile with the built-in assistant and your connections.

2. Build your list of acquaintances, allies, and advocates.

3. Formulate an action plan to develop and nurture your network.

How can you grow acquaintances into allies?

What is your plan of action?

4. The more you give, the more you get. So, the more you focus on building and nurturing your network, the more benefits you get. It is about putting your intention out there and allowing the universe to help you achieve it. You give more to the universe, and the universe will give more back to you. I can personally vouch for this from my experience.

5. When you have the lists of your acquaintances, allies, and advocates ready, connect with people from your organization straight away. They are more likely to accept the invitation because you are colleagues. You may need much of an introduction. A similar approach works with people from the same fraternity.

6. Nurture relationships, acknowledge their power, even if you do not want anything from them. The more you give, the more you get, as I said earlier. So, the more you offer your time and space, the more you get in return.

7. Finally, nurture your network when you do not need them, because when you do need them, they will be available to you for support.

Great careers are built on great values. Let us understand how to recognize our values and build our careers and relationships on the basis of these values.

"I am not a product of my circumstances. I am a product of my decisions."

– Stephen Covey

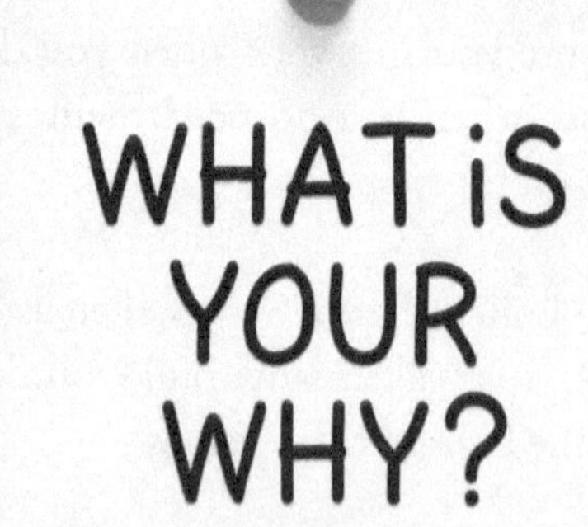
WHAT iS
YOUR
WHY?

CHAPTER

03
Values

Nothing is given to man on earth - struggle is built into the nature of life, and conflict is possible - the hero is the man who lets no obstacle prevent him from pursuing the values he has chosen.

– Andrew Bernstein

"I hope I don't see your face again!" she thundered. She flung the relieving letter she had just signed onto my table and stomped out. I picked up the letter, as I watched her exit the office. The boss had decided to let her go ostensibly due to adjustment issues. I had the task of conveying the message.

The incident set me thinking. How do you know who will turn out to be a good colleague or friend? Over a lifetime, we meet many people. We interact with them in childhood, and later, at work or in personal life. We get along with some and not so much with others. Some relationships continue to be maintained through life, and some do not. Circumstances change; people change. Change is constant. But values remain the same. Relationships can be built on values.

Leaders need to be aware of their values in order to build relationships. Recognizing a stakeholder's values is the next step, and this helps build relationships. One should also be aware of one's own emotional competence to deal with different kinds of situations. Recognizing one's own emotions, managing those emotions, recognizing others' emotions and managing their emotions is a leadership ability. This ability can be developed to a great degree, provided the awareness is built up.

WHAT ARE VALUES

Values are deeply held beliefs. We make our choices and decisions based on our values which guide us in all spheres of our lives. In all our actions and behaviours in any given situation, our values play an important role. In our work and in personal life, values give us much needed direction. When we are able to live according to our values, it finds meaning in our lives. This leaves us with a feeling of happiness and fulfilment. Ambition, punctuality, honesty, collaboration, integrity, challenge, service, friendship, transparency, independence and so on are examples of values. When we clarify our values to ourselves and practice our values, we are able to make better choices and priorities.

The more we internalise our values in day-to-day personal and professional life, the more we will be able to do what is important to us. Generally, a group of values provides us with our reference structure to operate in a general set of situations. Some values change and evolve as we mature, while others remain constant throughout our lives. When we make decisions in any situation, we invoke several of our values at the same time, either consciously or sub-consciously. Sometimes, our values operate below our general awareness. We need to bring these values out into our consciousness.

WHEN VALUES ARE IN CONFLICT

Sometimes we tend to feel misaligned in our interactions with others. In such situations of feeling inadequate and incomplete in our relationship with them it is possible that our personal values do not match those of the other individual. We feel that the conversation is not aligned to our intent. We might feel a certain incompleteness in the interaction and a lack of being in harmony with the other person. We might have a heated argument, even an all-out conflict. We may get anxious or upset or stressed and try to find ways to move the discussion forward. We may succeed in doing so, or we may not succeed. If we do not succeed, it is likely that relationships also may not succeed or progress beyond a point. Especially if the relationship is a close and personal one, we may hit a roadblock. If a work relationship has broken down or we do not feel happy or fulfilled at work, we may experience different feelings depending on the day, such as not wanting to show up for work on time, or not show up at all, or refuse to take on a particular project, or procrastinate despite an approaching deadline and so on. These are warning signs that your values are on conflict with those you experience at work and with colleagues or even your boss. It is possible to identify which values are in conflict however it takes some knowledge and practice to become aware of this in the moment. When you realise which values are in conflict you might take some steps to find common ground and move forward with better understanding. Going to work every day will not feel like a chore anymore.

A couple of examples will explain this: I had a manager who was friendly and easy going. He would review my performance and give me feedback as well as provide me enough freedom at work. With this manager I was able to identify that freedom at work, transparency, communication, proactiveness, structured work style were some of the values that we shared in common. These values were aligned and hence we had a healthy working relationship. Our relationship also had its share of intense moments, when I would mess up or something didn't quite go as planned. Even in such a situation, though the boss might take a difficult decision that one may not like, it would still be possible to see their point. Alignment in values, leads to a healthy working relationship which builds trust. I was happy working with this manager.

I had another manager in another organisation who was a quiet and intelligent, however did not provide me adequate feedback especially when I really needed it; there were occasions when I felt that he was not being fully transparent; instead, he was negative, overtly cautious and not very supportive of people development, or so I felt. I often had to get him to give me feedback by specifically asking for it. Note the way I just described my experience with that manager. I had a less than adequate experience with this manager and often felt stifled, suffocated and not acknowledged. What's more, I used to use my earlier experience as a point of reference when it came to benchmarking the values in alignment or misalignment. Which values do you think were in conflict here between my manager and myself? There seemed to be more values in conflict than those in alignment. The pertinent point here to think about is, what do you do in such a situation? How can one identify values in conflict and overcome them. Is it possible to overcome them. Jobs are not easy to come by always and adjustment with the environment may be needed depending on how ready the workplace (read colleagues, boss and other stakeholders) is for alignment to happen. There will be efforts needed to be taken by us as individuals since we have control only over ourselves.

EXTRINSIC AND INTRINSIC DRIVERS

Values can be leveraged to grow and sustain a relationship. For this to happen it is essential to understand our own values better. While some of us may be very clear about our values, for others, these values may not be readily identifiable or expressed. They may have been operating with their values without naming or labelling them as such. These values may be existing below the surface level of consciousness as demonstrated by the iceberg model. Imagine a ship, like the Titanic, cutting through the waters of the North Pacific Ocean on its voyage from Southampton England to New York, USA. A lookout on the ship spots an iceberg ahead. It may not have evoked any feeling of looming danger. However, if the lookout and the crew ignore the small portion of ice because of what they see above the surface of the water, they could run into trouble, because that bit of ice could be quite literally the proverbial 'tip of an iceberg'. An iceberg floats in water with a comparatively smaller portion above the surface of the water. A large mass of ice exists below the surface of the water, out of sight of the human eye, and this is potentially dangerous. Human interactions are similar. The iceberg model is often used to explain the different scenarios that are possible in human interaction. We do not see what we cannot see. What is hidden from our view and our understanding needs to be brought to the surface. These might be deeper issues such as beliefs, values and thought processes. If we do not consider the hidden drivers, we could potentially be assessing a situation or a person inaccurately and this could affect relationships.

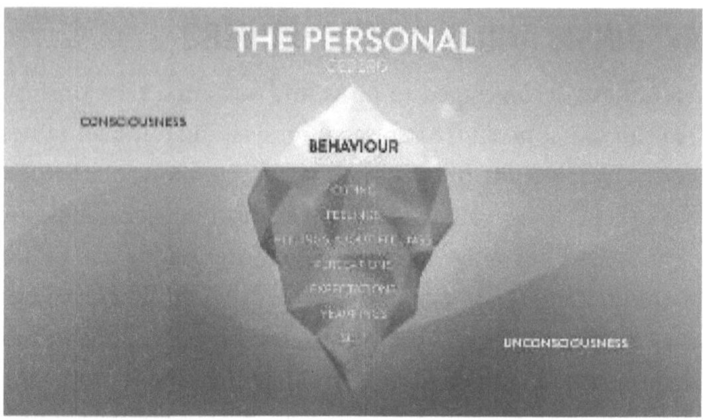

What is above the surface in human interaction, is visible to others such as our appearance, our body language, the way we talk and express ourselves. These can be revealing but can also be misleading. We respond to what we see above the surface of others. We consider the stimuli or triggers that we observe and create our own interpretations. In sensitive situations, these interpretations can lead to a variety of emotions, depending on the individual and the context. Based on the intensity of emotion - low or high - a behaviour is generated. What follows the behaviour is an outcome: a relationship is maintained, strengthened or strained. Therefore, for a more accurate response to a trigger, it may be worthwhile to examine not only the extrinsic drivers but also the intrinsic drivers.

What you can see and hear are the extrinsic drivers. These can be discussed and clarified. What we cannot see - what is below the surface - are the intrinsic drivers. To get a better understanding of what is below the surface of a personality, a good amount of self-awareness is needed.

BECOMING AWARE OF YOUR VALUES

I mentioned that our values sometimes exist below our level of awareness. In order to become aware of our values, we need to bring them to the surface of our consciousness. When our personal values do not match our organization's values, or a stakeholder's values, we somehow feel it within ourselves. We feel we are out of sync with what is happening in the moment. We find it a challenge to align with the other person's views, or become anxious or upset, sometimes even stressed or burnt out. We become apprehensive about how a particular transaction will happen, or how another one will progress. We are not sure whether we will be able to convince someone or convey our sense of discomfort. We know, deep within our bones, there is little or no connect with the other person. If we bring our values to our consciousness, we can identify the misalignments and work with them.

On the other hand, when we begin to live our values, we instinctively start to feel more comfortable with ourselves; our minds and bodies are in alignment.

We need to know ourselves well to be able to understand our values. How do we do that? A lot depends on our authenticity. Remember, the most significant influencers became so because of their authenticity – their ability to operate authentically from a values point of view. Strive to align your requests, transactions, words and statements with your values. It is not just about you and understanding your values; only when you understand your values will you begin to understand others' values.

Let's say you are creating a business proposal. The success of a proposal has a lot to do with integrity - integrity of people and processes. Say, integrity is an important part of your organization's rulebook and policies. You also know that your boss to whom you're presenting the proposal, highly values integrity in all its forms and manifestations. When you have this knowledge, it is easier for you to reference the value of integrity when you pitch the proposal and make it immediately recognizable for its alignment to the values. When values are in alignment, when two partners are able to align with each other's values, they begin to have more meaningful discussions, focused on a win-win outcome. That is why you must know your values. When you get used to recognizing your values, you will be able to identify and recognize others' values. You will begin to conduct your transactions based on those values, naturally seeking alignment wherever possible and wherever meaningful. You will find it easier to have a better working relationship as well as influence stakeholders better for a win-win.

RECOGNISING ALIGNMENT IN VALUES

Organisations, industries, professions and jobs operate on the basis of values, expressed or deemed. Personally, our values are most important to us. The intersection of values between us as individuals and the institutions we interact with is important to consider in that, the more there is common ground, the more we fit in. As simple as that.

People who seem to be living quiet, happy lives have possibly already identified their values and have consciously or unconsciously aligned them with colleagues at work and in their day-to-day lives. Even if some values are in conflict, it is possible that these individuals make adjustments in their day-to-day life, for the larger good, or for peaceful co-existence.

People who can live their values in the environments that they operate in are actually more productive. They are happier at work. If you find someone happy at work, you might immediately recognize that this person has been able to align his or her values with the those of their environment. The process of alignment is often a journey of discovery. Some get there early, others reach late. But a great objective to have in life is to understand and pursue our own values, and also acquire the ability to recognise those values in others.

IDENTIFYING OUR VALUES

We can assess our own values, identify our topmost ones, and then take steps to actually live out those values in a wholesome manner. When we try to sync our top ten values to our day-to-day actions, it tends to create a sense of harmony in our minds. We feel satisfied in our interactions with others. If there is an alignment of those values with the environment we work in, we feel comfortable, quite at peace with ourselves and the environment (See sample worksheets at the end of this chapter to help you in this regard.)

But if there is less alignment of our values with the environments we work in, the situation creates stress.

There is potential for conflict. These are people who experience discord between their values and the those of the environment they work in, or people they work with. When we are forced to operate with values that are not ours, stress, resistance and disharmony could result.

Our aim is to move closer and closer to aligning our values with those of our environment and our stakeholders: boss, organization, any colleague with whom there is a day-to-day interaction, that the individual interacts with, works with, or manages. For this to happen, we need to identify our own values, and then determine what actions we can take to live those values more thoroughly and more fully. The sample worksheets given at the end of this chapter will not only help you identify and discover your values, but help you recognise values in others, particularly stakeholders with whom you work on a regular basis.

RECOGNISE OTHERS' VALUES

The ability to recognise other's values comes with practise of mindfully calling out one's own values at work and in personal life. The better you know your values, the better you will be able to spot the values of your boss, your team members and others. It will then be easier for you to come to the same platform for communication.

APPRECIATION AS A VALUE

Appreciation is important in any relationship – whether in work relationships or personal relationships - not just as a nice-to-have, but an important communication essential, even considered an inter-personal skill.

In my training sessions I have posed several interesting questions and discussions surrounding stakeholder relationships and appreciation, and the views have been quite varied. In a class survey I conducted, 65% of my respondents said that appreciation is essential in both work and personal relationships. In comparison, 30% felt appreciation is necessary only in work relationships, and 5% found it essential only in personal relationships.

Appreciation is not regarded as a must-have amongst many managers, which is unfortunate. The reason why people are not so much into appreciating their team is possibly because of their own insecurities. This could also be a cultural issue, depending on the practices of the region they belong to. They may hold back from appreciating what they consider 'just routine work', or because they fear the person could get the 'wrong message', or that the team member may get too big for his boots. Well, if you refrain from appreciating someone thinking that the person will get too big for their boots, it is only a reflection of your inability to manage the stakeholder appropriate to the context, by managing your own insecurities.

The skill of appreciating is sometimes defined as 'recognising', but there is a subtle difference. 'Recognising' connotes an 'acknowledgement plus'. Recognizing simply helps build a better connect between employees without having to indulge in all-out praise.

WHY PEOPLE DO NOT APPRECIATE OTHERS

In the years I have spent within organisations, and surprisingly at senior levels sometimes, I have noticed that it is usually one's own insecurity that keeps them from appreciating others who have done a good job. Everyone likes appreciation. You can even express appreciation for your boss. It can be lonely at the top. They feel good about it, though some may not acknowledge it. However, do not overdo appreciation, or do it for the sake of a background agenda. A certain posturing can be at play in these situations. Appreciation or acknowledgement is feedback. And feedback is a gift. It is up to you how you want to treat it, whether you give it or receive it.

WHY WE SHOULD APPRECIATE OTHERS

"The deepest principle in human nature is the craving to be appreciated," said Dale Carnegie. Why is appreciation important? Well, the simple answer is, because we like being appreciated! We feel good being appreciated. When you become a manager, or a team leader, make sure you tell your team members that they did a good job. Remember, you wanted it when you were a team member. Pay it forward when you get a chance. And give it freely.

There's a scientific reason why appreciation makes a person feel good. It is all about neurochemistry. Appreciation sets off chemical reactions in our bodies. According to Dr. Judith Glaser, neuroscientist and author of the book: Conversational Intelligence, when we are appreciated or recognised, the hormone oxytocin is released in the brain, and our body and mind are wired to think, "Wow, when I did that, I got rewarded… it felt good". Therefore, the mind tends to repeat that action, as it seeks the good feeling again. So consequently, appreciation or recognition is a significant interpersonal skill, along with the skills of listening, questioning, building on the ideas of others, constructive argument, involving and so on. It helps build relationships.

STRENGTHENING RELATIONSHIPS

How do we analyse our relationships, identify strong and weak ones, and determine which ones, whether at work or at home, to focus on, to build and nurture? We need to first analyse the strength of our relationships using a sociogram technique which is explained at the end of this chapter.

Remember, this analysis works best for direct stakeholders – at work or in private life. It helps you know in an instant, which relationships are weaker than others which ones you might want to focus on first, to make them better, and identify values and communicate with them on the basis of those values, because you have common objectives with the stakeholder. You need to work together with your stakeholders. You cannot wish them away. You might as well improve your zigzag relationships to dotted line relationships or your dotted lines to solid lines to have a better working environment that supports better performance and therefore better satisfaction at work. You might also think that you really do not care for a specific line of relationship especially if it is zigzag or dotted line. Examine such relationships and question them yourself as to whether these are indeed stakeholder relationships or not. Very clearly, stakeholder relationships are exactly just that – you have a stake in that relationship, and it is important that the relationship is maintained healthy, adding value.

VALUES AND REJECTION

I recommend watching the TED Talk by Jia Jiang titled: What I learned from 100 days of Rejection (https://www. youtube.com/watch?v=-vZXgApsPCQ0). I'm sure all of you have felt rejected at some point in your life. You feel a little pain in your chest. It can feel like a vacuum. It is only natural that you feel rejection. We turn away from opportunities fearing rejection. Jia Jiang even terms rejection as his Bogeyman. However, you can overcome this fear of rejection. Jia Jiang says something wonderful. When you are faced with rejection, he says, do not run away from it. Do not reject it. Accept that the more you reject rejection, the more it will come back to haunt you. Rejection according to Jia can be handled by taking it head-on – feel it, experience it, embrace it, and let it go. Jia Jiang experimented with and experienced first-hand rejection multiple times. The initial few instances were awkward he says. He literally ran away from the scene. But later he got used to carrying rejection as his friend. After all, unless you get rejected how will you know about acceptance.

SAMPLE WORKSHEETS

IDENTIFYING YOUR VALUES

Here is a set of values. Read through these values and do the exercise that follows:

1. Entrepreneurship
2. Authority
3. Accountability
4. Financial Security
5. Trustworthiness
6. Safe Environment
7. Innovation
8. Cooperation
9. Continuous Improvement
10. Drive to Succeed
11. Control
12. Service
13. Expertise
14. Work-Life Balance
15. Routine
16. Order
17. Teamwork
18. Initiative
19. Generosity
20. Brevity
21. Spirituality
22. Tradition
23. Respect
24. Personal Security
25. Truthfulness
26. Playfulness
27. Predictability
28. Family
29. Honesty
30. Appreciation
31. Advancement
32. Sustainability
33. Security
34. Excellence
35. Variety
36. Structure
37. Friendship
38. Prestige
39. Strength
40. Fame
41. Job Security
42. Fairness
43. Creativity
44. Status
45. Autonomy
46. Wealth
47. Certainty
48. Compassion
49. Preservation
50. Goal Orientation
51. Recognition
52. Making a Difference
53. Safety
54. Integrity
55. Learning
56. Health
57. Kindness
58. Curiosity
59. Detail
60. Humour

Recall your best work experience in your life and career so far. From the list above identify five values that were present in that 'best' work experience.

Now cast your mind to your worst work experience. Which five values on the list above were missing in that experience? Write them down.

Now you have five values that were present in the best work experience and five values that were missing from your worst work experience. You now have a list of ten values altogether that are important to you. There might be more.

Think of people around you. They could be anyone - a classmate, a colleague or a boss, your, father, mother, brother, sister, partner, friend… Write down their names and write a value or two that you recognise in them. Their values need not match the values you have identified for yourself. What matters here is how their values have impacted you.

Remember, this is an ever-evolving process, and you might add more to this list as the years progress. Five years down the line, rethink these questions and answer them. You would have been enriched with more intense work experiences. This is life. Life is full of challenges. You will have different types of experiences. Update your list of values periodically. Identify your top ten values each time and see how you evolve.

STRENGTHENING OUR RELATIONSHIPS – THE SOCIOGRAM

Take your notepad and pen. Draw a small circle in the middle of the sheet and write your name in it. Then list eight to ten stakeholders at work by the side of the sheet. You can do this exercise for personal stakeholders separately. Draw small circles around the one with your name, leaving some space between 'your circle' and the others arranged around it.

Now draw lines from 'your circle' to each stakeholder's circle. The type of line will indicate the strength of your relationship with that stakeholder. You can draw a solid line or a dotted line or a zigzag line, depending on how strong or weak your relationship is with that stakeholder. (Refer the picture).

If you have a solid or strong relationship – draw a solid line.

If you have a so-so relationship, neither strong nor weak – draw a dotted line.

If you have a weak relationship – draw a zigzag line.

TAKEAWAYS

BENEFITS OF KNOWING VALUES

Knowing our values as much as possible, helps us choose the best possible environment to live or work in. We have to know our values in order to determine whether the person or the people we are going to work with share those same values. Now you might ask: "how can I find out whether the people I'm going to work with share the same values?" Well, it is possible to do that.

All of us have a hierarchy of values and a certain natural prioritisation of those values. The ranking of values that exists within needs to be brought to the fore.

Which values do you use effectively in your solid line connections, which can be used to convert dotted and zig-zag relationships into solid ones?

Examples of values: Collaboration, Open communication, Avoiding Judgement.

Examples of skills: Listening fully before responding, asking open questions etc.

How do you identify with the values you have discovered through the exercise?

Which ones would you like to live 'more fully'?

What would you like to do, to live them more fully?

Read this aloud like a mantra:

"Everything I desire is within me; today and every day, I give that which I want to receive."

This is a mantra from Dr. Deepak Chopra's meditation sessions. The more you are sincere about your intentions, the more the universe conspires to make that happen, according to Wayne Dwyer in The Power of Intention. Desire connection, desire value-based relationships, you will acquire these and much more.

The more you give, the more you get.

I give that which I want to receive. If I do not give, how can I expect to receive?

There is much give-and-take in all relationships. It is a great value to build on. The more you give, the more you get. Merging learnings in the previous chapter on Networking, the more you nurture your network, the more you can expect from it. The more you give, the more you get.

CALL TO ACTION

Use your values to recognise others' values.

Do the sociogram for your family members and your work peers.

Look at how can you enhance your relationship from zigzag to dotted and dotted to solid lines.

What are you going to do about your fear of rejection? That answer can only be found after you watch the video.

"Keep your thoughts positive because your thoughts become your words. Keep your words positive because your words become your behaviour. Keep your behaviour positive because your behaviour becomes your habits. Keep your habits positive because your habits become your values. Keep your values positive because your values become your destiny."

– Mahatma Gandhi

CHAPTER

04

Leader

"Before you are a leader, success is all about growing yourself. When you become a leader, success is all about growing others."

– Jack Welch

"Una mattina mi sono alzato

O bella ciao, bella ciao, bella ciao, ciao, ciao

Una mattina mi sono azalto

E ho trovato l'invasor

O partigiano, portami via

O bella ciao, bella ciao, bella ciao, ciao, ciao

O partigiano, portami via

Ché mi sento di morir…"

Title song from the Netflix series, *La Casa de Papel* or *Money Heist*.

Roughly translated the song means:

"One morning, I got up, O beautiful, hello, beautiful, hello, beautiful, hello, hello, hello,

One morning, I got upset, And I found the invader…

O partisan, take me away, O beautiful hello, beautiful hello, beautiful hello, hello, hello,

O partisan, take me away, Because I feel like I'm going to die…"

'Bella ciao', Italian for 'goodbye beautiful' is "an Italian protest folk song that originated in the hardships of the mondina women, the paddy field workers in the late 19th century who sang it to protest against harsh working conditions in the paddy fields of Northern Italy." (Wiki).

The Money Heist (La Casa de Papel) adopted this folk song to provide its story line a flavour of resistance, played during big plot moments on the show, and today used worldwide as a hymn of freedom, a song of solidarity. The series itself reveals lessons on leadership, of working in teams and organizations albeit in an elaborate robbery project.

Recently I recalled the lessons one can learn from this series having watched the initial episodes in Spanish since 2017 when it was first released as a Spanish TV series. The series was wildly popular in its storyline as well as its suspense, as it portrayed the strategies and failures of leadership, challenges in managing a team of experts with varied expertise, and in forming teams with shared goals, shared values and shared culture.

The story is about a gang of initially eight people and their motivations to plan and carry out the largest heist in history. Led by the 'Professor' who carves the strategy and meticulously plans the entire operation as well as trains this exclusive group of handpicked men and women for 5 months in the countryside near Madrid. The plan is to enter the Royal Mint of Spain, ensure no staff leave, and print 240 billion euros, how many ever days it takes. A heist is a crime. But the heist in itself has become a documentary film on leadership and management.

In case you read the previous chapter on values, it might be worth recalling some key takeaways that help us understand the value of relationship as a means of learning leadership better. Whether you try upgrading your zigzag line relationships to dotted or solid line relationships, or internally establish the connection between values and authenticity, or identify your individual values and how to leverage them, or how to recognize your counterpart's values - all of these move you a few steps closer to becoming a better leader.

A leader is constantly motivated to improve and maintain relationships within the team. Most leaders I have worked with find the exercise of identifying their values a great start. They go about examining how to leverage them within the teams they lead. Identifying your values by using your good experiences and not-so-good experiences, to find out which values were present or which values were not present, is a great way by which to identify what is important for you. Let us now look at what it takes to be a great leader.

LEADERSHIP LESSONS

Here are some leadership lessons I have learnt. The fantastic stories, script and direction of Money Heist stimulated my thinking on these lessons that I now share with you. Years down, the series may still be popular or may be forgotten, but these lessons are evergreen.

A BURNING DESIRE

I am a great fan of a leader having a 'burning desire', a term I borrow from Napoleon Hill (in Think and Grow Rich).

Firstly, for any intention, be it career growth, pursuance of a life goal or simply achieving a milestone, we are driven primarily by a desire. The difference between a desire and a burning desire is tremendous. A desire can be scuttled merely by a disappointing obstacle or unexpected roadblock. A burning desire is necessary in order to achieve a planned degree of success. We all have it in us – but to varying levels. In the Money Heist series, the 'Professor' had a grave desire behind the heist. He was paying homage to his father, who died working as a bank robber to treat his ill son, the young Sergio. Sergio is the 'professor' and the brain behind the heist. His vision of his complex mission was to be able to recreate a real heist, with meticulous planning and a team of committed gang members. What is interesting is, besides the morality factor of whether it is 'right' to rob a mint, is also about looking at the story as a piece of moral art – the Professor had a sort of Robinhood image of stealing from the rich to benefit the poor, or not stealing at all as he was minting his own money.

A burning desire is what makes the difference between success and failure. In business, it is said that 90% of startups fail in the first year of business operations. There are several reasons why that happens. One common pitfall is procrastination - not taking decisions, delaying taking decisions or worse - not implementing decisions taken, because of the fear of failure and other insecurities. Napoleon Hill said 'desire is the first step towards riches. You've got to have a desire – and a burning desire at that. Now, while some people desire to possess riches, others desire to keep adding value to what they do. The indirect outcome of doing what you do and doing it well is riches in due course.

Any way you look at it, it could be a direct objective, or it could be an indirect objective. It really does not matter. Different people are motivated by different things. Either way, you have got to have a burning desire to do something to move. Pursue your objective to pursue your targets to pursue your goals. *If your journey is not fuelled by a burning desire to succeed, you may not last through the pursuance of that goal.* Many people pursue their goals and desires and depend on accident or providence to make it. These goals may not necessarily be 'must-haves', they might be 'nice-to-haves'. The idea of a 'must-have' or a 'nice-to-have' is entirely up to the goal-owner.

"When you set an intention, when you commit, the entire universe conspires to make it happen," says Sandy Forster. Dr. Wayne W. Dyer makes the distinction in his book 'The Power of Intention': He says that it all depends on the strength of your intention. It depends on the strength of your burning desire, that your reality will be created. "Once you make a decision, the universe will conspire to make it happen," says Ralph Waldo Emerson. If you have a strong intention, and you put that intention out into the universe, the universe ensures to make it happen. Things have a way of happening at the right place and at the right time. Don't you think?

Have you not had an experience where you have let's say, been working on an important project for days and the required resources, people, events and so on suddenly seem to be happening to you contributing to your progress? People who have had that burning desire are those people you might see today as being successful and stable entrepreneurs. There is always a story behind successful entrepreneurs. Not everyone has been successful. There are people who have made silly mistakes and have lost billions of dollars. Elon Musk. One day, a tweet was all it took for his stock prices to come crashing down. But he is still pretty much up there though he almost got the sack from his own company. There are several stories about fatal mistakes, very small mistakes that have scuttled big plans. A burning desire is an absolute important factor in this whole pursuit of one's own intention and one's own desire, pursuing one's own targets and objectives.

VISUALISING

Visualization is powerful. Steven Covey describes visualising your destination as the second habit in his book the Seven Habits of Highly Effective People. Habit number two says, 'begin with the end in mind'. Visualize that scene in which you have achieved your goal.

In chapter 1, I asked you to attempt to write down a personal vision. One of the following might be true for you: Your personal vision statement is probably easy to write on the go, or you may write it down but with some difficulty. It is possible you cannot think of a vision at the moment, or you do not have a vision yet. Some may feel that their vision (in their opinion) is impossible to achieve, while others might already be witnessing their vision taking shape! Whatever your situation, at any point of time, arriving at a visual of the ultimate destination of an individual could be painfully intriguing or a blissfully simple exercise.

And if you do have a vision statement written down, you might even ask yourself, "does this sound good enough?

Is it meaningful? Does it make sense?" and so on. Many of us want to know if it 'looks' good enough, or whether it makes sense for themselves! Worry not. A meaningful personal vision depends on the meaning you make of it. At this point you need to let go of the need for a good-looking vision statement, which I read as one that gets the approval of others – something we are wired for from school - and begin to accept your own thinking as being authentic and real. The meaning you make of it, and what you have in mind as a personal destination is good for your vision. You may visualize an entire scene, context or environment that you can describe peering into your mind's eye, an entire scenario that you would like your life's efforts to leave to your journey to lead to. For some of you it is quite specific. And that's perfect. For others, you might have just started thinking of a vision, a goal or an ambition. Personally, I did not have my personal vision defined when I started my career. I did not even have It when I was HR Director at the age of 39. My vision got to be crafted, though not so perfectly, when I started my second career at age 42. Therefore, it began taking shape only a few years ago. Does that mean I spent 20 years of my career without a vision? Not necessarily. I did have a goal – to get to the highest level in my profession – to head the HR function. I achieved that position. Thereafter, I had a need to start defining a more concrete vision. I took the help of a coach to guide the process of defining my personal vision statement. My vision chart is just about eight years old now. Is it relevant still? I more and more believe it is. What I have done in the last 8 years is a great validation to the vison I laid for myself – "to help leaders achieve sustained change in behaviours, to enhance their professional and personal success."

A great revelation to me was that whatever I was doing throughout my career and probably right from the start was a natural, intrinsic process of building towards this statement I would draft nearly 20 years after I started my career. This is probably what I wanted to do but did not know the right words to define it. Not until a coach guided me to put it down in words and in pictures. And that is when I realized, wow, this is what I want to do. I could not voice it to anybody.

So, if somebody asks you to define your personal vision it is not necessary that you must come up with the perfect definition. If you have a "visualization" in your mind of what that scenario looks like, where you find yourself in X number of years, that is the first step. You need to fix your destination. Alice in *Alice in Wonderland* asked the cat she met on her journey, which path she should take? And the cat said, 'well that depends on where you want to go.' Alice replied, 'I don't much care where I want to go.' The cat said, 'then it doesn't really matter which path you take.' You need to know what destination you would like to pursue, or at least a direction you would like to take. That is visualization. It is powerful.

PLANNING

The third lesson is to plan masterfully. The professor in *Money Heist* is a seasoned chess player. His power to plan the tiniest details to the highest order is a product of the two previous practices that he had. He had some dry runs. We have dry runs for every project, to make sure nothing is left to chance. You need to have a team working behind the scenes. They listen and look out for possible issues in team delivery. You need a bird's eye-view of the entire project. You can't organize your chessboard if you can't see all the pieces, so therefore, it's very important to have a helicopter view or a bird's eye view of your plan. If a builder wants to build a building, they make a 'plan' first. They want to see how the building would look like, what is going to be the structure, and how it is going to look like in the end. They start with the plan and then lay the first brick of the foundation. The more solid your plans, the less problems you will face in the future. The professor in *Money Heist* had a plan A, a plan B, a Plan C, and maybe a plan D as well. Nothing was left to chance.

LEADERSHIP

All of that builds into leadership – the skills that will come in handy that build on the other allied skills. Train and motivate your employees to handle the part of operation that you can delegate. Just remember that leadership starts with yourself first. Leadership starts with you and in you. When you become a leader of a team, or whether you are an individual contributor, remember, you are a leader of opportunities to display your leadership. When you are in an impromptu group like a training group and you are suddenly made the coordinator of a breakout group, you become a sort of 'peer leader'. These people don't report to you, but you have a coordination responsibility. And that is a leadership responsibility yet keeping a team member role. You do not have to always be the team leader. Leadership can be displayed by being an effective team member. Leadership can be displayed even if you are an individual contributor.

BUILDING YOUR BRAND

Building your brand is a self-leadership skill. Branding yourself with your unique contribution, your unique abilities and your unique way. The professor on *Money Heist* branded his way to the team's heart. It takes a discipline to follow through on your plans and ideas however minor or major. That builds your brand. One important part of the success of the heist was to avoid any bloodshed. The professor had the most serious face when he addressed the team saying, the second any blood is shed, we will no longer be Robin Hood, but a bunch of plain punks. What is the difference between a bunch of plain punks and a gang that is trying to cultivate a cult persona of a 'Robin Hood'. We are here as Robin Hood; we have come into plunder and loot and distribute the spoils to the poor and common people. They wanted to project the Robin Hood persona which would be possible only if they made sure that there is no bloodshed. Nobody is killed. The gang had very serious instructions that they should not shoot the police or even the hostages. Personal branding is a frontier for entrepreneurship. Freedom encompasses how the customer sees and defines you.

CONSISTENCY

Consistency pays. If you start a new habit, be consistent, and you are going to solidify those habits into a routine action. When the initial awkwardness of a new habit wears off, it becomes a way of doing things. All you need to do then is just implement - just do it. Jim Rohn said, 'success is neither magical nor mysterious. Success is the natural consequence of consistently applying basic fundamentals. These are all basic fundamentals. Being on time is a basic fundamental. Getting into the habit of being on time will do great things for your career. One of the biggest early career lessons that I learned working in a global German organization is this: you should never be on time. Ever. You should be *before time*. Because when you are before time you allow for surprises along the way, that could hold you back from being on time. A matter of caution: there are people who might say, why so early? Why do you want to go so early? Ignore them. They are not the ones who are impacted; therefore, they would not fully absorb the consequences of being delayed or late. It is okay to be abnormally early than risk being late.

PERSISTENCE

Persistence pays. No matter how many tactics were employed by the Spanish police, 'Berlin' always said 'we stick to the plan'. Stick to the plan, stick to the script, stick to the process. No shortcuts. We have a plan A, we have a plan B, we have a plan C and a plan D. We have left nothing to chance. And in the event of that 1% chance of something going wrong that we haven't thought of, there is still a plan E. This is like all high-performance teams – the Navy SEALS, the FIFA top ten teams as examples – they leave nothing to chance. Overcoming hardship is what separates the entrepreneurs and career professionals from the wannabe-preneurs. A leader thinks like an entrepreneur. My team. My business. My leadership. The entrepreneur spirit of thinking like an entrepreneur is when you have the whole organization's perspective very clearly in your mind – overall goals and outcomes.

KEEPING THE FAITH

Faith goes a long way. When communication between the professor and the team was cut off or stalled in *Money Heist* – and that did happen quite a few times, faith in the leader played a great role. The team operated with the faith that the leader will be back. I will come back, he said. In the training, they were told 'if you do not get to hear from me or if you do not see me, I'll be back'. He was operating remote control. He was not on the scene. He was outside in hiding. The instruction merely was, if I'm not reachable, wait for me to get back.

FINDING THE BALANCE

Gary Vaynerchuk says, most entrepreneurs today are entitled, that is a big problem. Entitlement interferes with your faith because you expect success as soon as you start. If you are just into your career for a few months or a year or two, do not take for granted, the successes that you have had or the authority that you have acquired or been handed down as though you are at the epitome of your career. Instead, build on them. The best is yet to come. Know that you have an entire career ahead, you are yet to see life enough and face myriad challenges that will further strengthen your mettle. There are many more previously unheard of and unseen challenges and problems that are going to be thrown at you throughout career. Wait for them, watch out for them, embrace them and overcome them. The successes or achievements that you have had in the first few months or years of your career are certainly going to stand you in good stead to handle bigger issues later on. Do not let success get into your head. Watch out for these pitfalls.

Remember we said earlier that problems need to be looked at as challenges. The more you look at them as challenges, the more you could convert them into opportunities. And that depends on your outlook - the way you look at problems. It is like looking at the glass half-empty versus looking at the same glass and saying, it is half-full. If you want to win the long game, have faith in what you are doing and enjoy the process of everyday hustle and find the right balance. The professor had a lot on his hands in orchestrating the heist. The group dynamics or the team dynamics needed to be managed. There were people within the team who were trying to become leaders, because they are all completely focused on the objective, they are all extremely motivated people, and they were accomplished experts in their own right. You could see that he made time for not only working out on the operations, but also for love. Look at the kind of work-life balance that he had. We need to strike the right balance between work and personal time. Those who are workaholic justify everything by being busy or are prone to becoming emotionally drained. Avoid getting hooked on to anything and eventually quit. People say I love my company. I would say, love your job. Work to provide value. Positions, titles, jobs, organizations, bosses, and salaries are all variable. What is constant is you, your performance and the value that you add – your contribution. Your personal time is important to you.

SYNERGY

The synergy of a mastermind is a leadership quality. Berlin and Palermo are planning the heist. They said 'if we use talent and science, the best minds in engineering, in physics, in fluid mechanics… Can you imagine them preparing for a job? Excellence supplied to a robbery. The dictionary defines synergy as the cooperation of two or more organizations, substances or other agents to produce a combined effect, which is greater than the sum of their separate effects. So united we stand, divided we fall. When we are united, the force multiplier of that unity is much stronger than the individual components. That is what where the basis of a team comes from. The foundation of a performing team is the synergy that a leader is able to bring in and have the team absorb and benefit from bonding.

Which of these five leader lessons are impacting you at the moment? The burning desire, the visualization, the planning, the leadership, leader branding, consistency, persistence, faith, balance, synergy, which of these are impacting you now? Which would be your top two action takeaways from *money heist*?

When I polled this question amongst a group of young professionals, most had chosen 'planning' as their topmost takeaway. Followed by having a burning desire you have got to have the planning necessary to take the first step. Then you're well on your way towards achieving your goal in a timeframe of your choosing. All ingredients we discussed in this chapter are important. It all starts with the burning intention and visualising your goal. Make your plans, your plan, your practice with your plan A, Plan B, Plan C, plan D, your necessary backup plans.

SUMMARY

- Burning Desire (Napoleon Hill): A passionate, unwavering commitment to achieving a specific goal. This desire is so strong that it drives you to take persistent and focused action.

- Intention (Wayne Dyer): The alignment of your personal will with a universal force, made stronger by a burning desire that focuses and energizes your intention.

- Visualizing your goal

- Planning your steps

- Leading yourself and leading others

- Building your brand

- Consistency in efforts

- Persistence pays

- Keeping the faith in the face of setbacks

- Finding the balance, not declaring success too early

- Synergy with stakeholders is key

CALL TO ACTION

Back to the drawing board with your pen and paper. What is your burning desire? Think about it, reflect on it, write it down. If you have written your personal vision, now funnel it and narrow down to what your burning desire looks like. It could be a part of the vision or the first major (or minor) step.

Number two, apply as many of the ten lessons as possible in a project that you might be managing or will be a part of soon. Your objective is to look at what lessons can you showcase from your learning in this chapter? What has been your experience so far? What have you discovered about yourself? And what have you learned?

You can form a team of six or seven members and have a plan do some great activities in line with existing objectives or something totally new. Come up with ideas, come up with a great innovative creative project.

Remember, problems should be looked at as challenges and convert them into opportunities. There may be a fear of trying. Make sure that you try anyway, you might win some you might lose some, but at least you have learned something out of it. Always be shameless and fearless to learn.

"*Leadership is not something you do to people; it's something you do with people.*"

"*The best leaders are those who understand that their role is to serve others, not to be served.*"

— Ken Blanchard

CHAPTER

05
Presence

'Presence is confidence without arrogance.'

– Amy Cuddy

I detest walking into a meeting after the meeting has started. When you do so, remember how everyone turns and stares at you? The meeting leader might also enthusiastically call you out by name and say, "welcome, welcome, would someone please give offer them a seat, thank you very much…" - and everyone would be shifting around trying to accommodate you, still staring. I detested crowds with peering eyes. And on top of that it is certainly embarrassing to be late for a meeting. Now years later, I am wiser. Being 'on time' is no longer sought after. Being 'before time' is the mantra. I fixed that first. If I cannot be on or before time, I prefer not to go. The peering eyes do not worry me anymore; I love them. I tell myself that they probably think I'm a star of some sort. My mindful presence creates that feeling in me - and my resultant body language hopefully delivers a more appropriate perception in them. This chapter deals techniques that will go a long way to help you craft your personal presence by dealing with your own mind first.

WHY IS PRESENCE IMPORTANT?

One day you suddenly get some feedback: *"You need to improve your executive presence."* What does it mean? What do I need to do? How will I know if I have it? Can I feel it? Is it a behaviour? Is it practical to gain Presence? And, who's defining Presence? Successful executives build up a reasonable amount of presence over the years by recognizing what works to gain attention with a variety of personalities and adapting themselves accordingly. People train themselves over the years and repeat certain beneficial behaviours through their experiences and these become habits. There are image consultants who teach how to enhance your presence. Professional image consultants teach, train and coach in building presence. They have a range of services from grooming your personality to enhancing your dress-sense, your body language and so on.

HOW TO GAIN PRESENCE

Harvard professor Amy Cuddy, through her research has written a book - *Presence: Bringing Your Boldest Self to Your Biggest Challenges*. She says, 'quiet confidence is the best'. Now, you might be a little confused with people who are loud, boisterous, and all over the place - and we think this is 'presence'. It is not necessarily so.

Let us get into the detail, dissecting 'presence' step by step to see what really makes up for 'presence' and what really builds up 'executive presence'. Amy Cuddy says, 'presence is confidence without arrogance'. We see people around who *try* to make their presence felt. You know them in an instant, be they world leaders, celebrities, or influencers. 'Sadly, confidence is often confused with cockiness.' 'The truly present executive is one who does not need to trumpet his or her achievements,' says Cuddy. Now, here's something I want to clarify: in our childhood years, growing up, you might recall teachers in school who tell children who may often talk about themselves and their achievements: "Do not boast! Boasting is a bad habit." When we start our careers, we come across trainers, coaches and motivational gurus who tell us, "You have to broadcast your achievements - get noticed, to win those promotions and rewards." Young adults are often confused by this paradox. Which one holds good? Cuddy says, 'the truly present executive is one who doesn't need to trumpet their achievements!' That's the balance that we are trying to make. Over the years I have realized that you need to trumpet your achievements. There is probably a better way to do it. You must be visible; and known for your contributions and for your performance. The boss must know who you are. It is good to stand out in a crowd if you can manage it – but not to obsess over it. Do what it takes to be in the limelight in a truly present way, not necessarily in a way that would distract or detract people, especially the ones you want to influence positively. People are generally wary of someone who is always trying to 'show off' or trying to make themselves heard all the time.

Your achievements will speak for themselves when presented in the right occasions. Present them where they help bring greater awareness to your strengths. For example, in an appraisal meeting or a promotion interview, or in a situation where you have a formal meeting and might want to make it known that you are responsible for an event, a successful activity or a progress achieved. This might help the course of the discussion and make way for better outcomes. Be subtle yet sure, and they would love you for your quiet confidence, your humility. One needs to be boldly humble, and courageously subtle. Be confident, be humble, and strike a balance. Let us break down what Amy Cuddy says further. The moment we break it down and look at those ingredients we can find out what it takes to be truly present.

CHANGE OTHER PEOPLE'S PERCEPTIONS WITH BODY LANGUAGE

Amy Cuddy, in her research on body language reveals that "we can change other people's perceptions, and even our own body chemistry simply by changing body positions". Cuddy provides a process with some simple steps to follow. Body language shapes who you are. Your body language gives you a channel to communicate. Everyone observes body language, however subtle. It is easy to pick up those subtle hints. People usually pick up these subtle signals and you might be transmitting a lot of messages that if you knew, you might change. It might be a whole volume of things that you really did not intend to express – just by giveaways like those your body signals in a conversation of transaction. That speaks a lot without the actual words. Actual words in verbal communication do much less. According to research, people use 65% non-verbal communication and only 35% verbal communication. In Dr. Albert Mehrabian's 7-38-55, *Rule of Personal Communication* the percentage of body language in communication is 55% as against 38% comprising voice and tone and only 7% in spoken words. Nagesh Belludi in his article says that 'the non-verbal elements are particularly important for communicating feelings and attitude. When they are incongruent, that is, if words and body language disagree, one tends to believe the body language. If a speaker's words and body language differ, listeners are more likely to believe the nonverbal communication of the speaker - not his words. Suppose someone says, "I don't have a problem with you!" while avoiding eye-contact, looking anxious, and maintaining a closed body language, irrespective of the person's internal dialogue, the listener will probably trust the predominant form of communication,' which according to Prof. Mehrabian's findings is non-verbal (38% + 55%), rather than the literal meaning of the words (7%).

So how do professional speakers and political leaders command presence in their arena of activity? To get answers Amy Cuddy studied the animal kingdom. Her research led her to find that animals have a certain body language when they are on a high or indicating victory and revert to another style when they feel vulnerable or fearful. The victory stance, such as a gorilla beating its chest or a rooster crowing, standing tall and erect, communicates authority, power or victory - 'I'm in charge', 'I'm responsible', 'I am stronger' and so on. For those feeling vulnerable, insecure or stressed before the start of a social event, a presentation meeting, or an appraisal discussion, Amy Cuddy recommends practicing a victory stance for two minutes – by simply stretching your hands high above your head in a victory stance. Feel that nervousness slipping away and a new feel of personal power pervading you. The moment you do this as well as take in a couple of deep breaths, you are breathing in more oxygen. You are also having a release of oxytocin, which is the positive chemical - a release of oxytocin in your brain. Your nervousness comes down, because oxytocin is up-regulated, and cortisol is down-regulated. When oxytocin is released in your brain, it also opens up your brain to ideas, creativity, innovation. You also begin to get ideas about how do I present my proposal? How do I meet them? How do I answer questions? What do I say first? What is the worst that can happen? You know, all of those positive reinforcing thoughts come into your mind, and then you would do a much better job the moment you get into this practice.

Years ago, as I was beginning my training career, I had to face international audiences, or even home crowds, and they it would freak me out. The one thing I tried doing to reduce my inner fear before such meetings was take a few mindful breaths and do some mindfulness exercises such as *pranayama*, calming my mind and building positive thoughts. I would then have a much better experience at the program feeling more relaxed, refreshed, and with renewed energy.

"Our bodies, change our minds, and our minds change our behaviour, and our behaviour changes our outcomes." - Amy Cuddy, *Presence: Bringing Your Boldest Self to Your Biggest Challenges*

The moment you indulge in a feel-good, positive, physical activity, the body responds in a positive way, sending messages to your mind encouraging you to think of your personal power, feel positive, giving you thoughts on how to face the situation at hand. The mind begins to change the behaviour - the actions that we take, walking erect and not slouching, speaking more confidently. Consequently, your body language begins to look much more positive than it originally was. When you physically do this, you begin to take control of your thoughts and actions. The mind immediately changes, the behaviour also follows, and the body language changes overall. You end up giving out more positive signals. When you start giving out positive signals, you find that positive signals are mirrored back to you.

When I meet a crowd for the first time in a training session I facilitate, there is always nervousness initially, that happens to just about anybody. Charlie Chaplin, the celebrated comedian and entertainer was such an accomplished actor but was said to be extremely nervous even before his 5000th performance on Broadway. However, when he was out on the stage, under the bright stage lights, he was a transformed man delivering his most stellar performances – and no one would see the nerves. When I initially stepped out on to the stage, I used to have nerves as well. A host of 30 or 50, poker-faced, strange, unknown faces would just stare back at me. One of the things that I found useful to do as soon as I get to see my audience is – smile. I would sweep my gaze slowly from left to right - and from right to left – silently making eye contact, genuinely smiling at all of them, telling myself that I love what I see. What do you think happens next? It's like magic mirror. They smile back at me. What is the mind telling me? These are friends! I have found this a great way to gain confidence at the start of a presentation. I tell my class that even if you have a poker-faced senior executive in the room who doesn't flinch at any emotion, do not worry. He is smiling on the inside, and I believe that. In much the same way, your nerves are not 'visible' outwardly to your audience. You rarely look as nervous as you feel! You and only you know your current state of mind. So, change your state of mind by using a physical action – such as a victory stance or a smile. And if your audience is still not smiling, silently smile back, smile again, continuously looking them in the eye until they smile back at you.

When Amy Cuddy gave her TED Talk on Presence, she observed, that to have the audience coming in and participating is very theatrical. She wanted to start by offering them a free, no-tech life hack. She said, "all it requires of you is that you change your posture for two minutes. Do a little audit of your body and what you're doing with your body. How many of you are sort of making yourself small, smaller, maybe your hunching, crossing your legs, maybe wrapping your ankles." Sometimes we hold on to our arms as if we are cold. Sometimes we spread out. Pay attention to what you are doing right now, it could significantly change the way your life unfolds. We are really fascinated with body language, and we are particularly interested in other people's body language. An awkward interaction or a smile or a contemptuous glance or a very awkward wink, even something like a handshake, says Amy, is very revealing. A handshake or the lack of a handshake between celebrities can have us talking for weeks, even with the BBC and the New York Times reporting it!

Nonverbal behaviour is language and therefore an integral part of communication. When we think about communication, we think about interactions. What is your body language communicating to me? What is mine communicating to you? Social scientists spend a lot of time looking at the effects of our body language on others or other people's body language on us. We make judgments and inferences from body language. Those judgments can predict meaningful life outcomes – 'like who we hire or promote, who we ask out on a date'. "If we go digital, emoticons used well in online negotiations can lead you to claim more value from that negotiation," says Amy Cuddy. "If you use them poorly, the outcomes are there to see. In the animal kingdom, it is about expanding. They make yourself big, they stretch out, they take up space, and are basically opening up, like a gorilla or a python. Humans do the same thing. They do this both when they when they have power sort of chronically, and also when they're feeling powerful in the moment."

Amy also suggests that research interestingly shows us how universal and old these expressions of power are. Jessica Tracy has studied people who are born with sight and people who are congenitally blind do the victory stance when they win at a physical competition. When they cross the finish line and they have won, it does not matter if they have never seen anyone do it, they also display the victory stance. Amy asks, 'what do we do when we feel powerless?' We do exactly the opposite. We close up, we wrap ourselves up, we make ourselves small, we don't want to bump into the person next to us. Both animals and humans do the same thing. This is what happens when you put together high and low power. What we tend to do when it comes to power is that we compliment the others' nonverbals. If someone is being really powerful with us, we tend to make ourselves smaller, we don't mirror them, we do the opposite of them."

I have watched behaviour in the classroom. I have noticed that students can express a lot of nonverbal power. The loud and outgoing ones can come into the room getting straight into the middle of the room before class starts and want to occupy the space that is most visible. They sit down, spread all out, expanding in their space and gesture wildly. You have other people who are coming in with visibly low energy, their facial expressions and bodies showing some stress. They sit in their chair, try to make themselves small, and raise their hands just a wee bit.

If we want to change the way we appear to the world, can we fake the body language? Can you smile, just for a little while, and actually experience a behavioural outcome that makes you seem more powerful? That was my experience with the audience and my own nerves. We know that our nonverbals govern how other people think and feel about us. But the question really is, do our nonverbals govern how we think and feel about ourselves?

That is the question I would like to leave with you. To bring about presence it is important to realize that a lot has got to do with body language. When the body changes, the mind follows, and the changed behaviour results. That is also why it may not be a challenge for many acquire it. You just have to nudge your body to do something, move your hand in a particular way, smile at an audience, and that sort of thing. The first few times would feel a bit awkward. Later the body would get used to it because the mind accepts the positive signals and your body language changes. The behaviours change and the outcome changes. This is what the expression, 'fake it till you make it' means. It is a new and deliberate bodily change that slowly becomes a part of you when you get used to it.

THE BODY, MIND, AND SOUL CONNECTION

It is about being in the moment, being mindful. You begin to become aware of your own physical presence and your thoughts before you go to a meeting or a presentation. You are connecting the body, mind, and soul. You are back in control of yourself, managing your nerves better. It feels wholesome. Your presence is an output of who you are and what you create. By soul, we mean believing in yourself, the power and the spirit that resides in you. Tap it, recognizing it, and then your mind. Practice focus. Focus on your body and your actions being mindful of what you are doing. Let your body perform. When soul and your mind are connected, focus, and the power is tapped. You must focus on the practice of how your behaviour, actions, statements stand strong during challenges, performing at their best. Now with all these, believe that there is a Way. Also remember, that when your creative expressions match the needs of those around you, you're allowing the universe to work through you. The abundance effortlessly flows into your life in perfect order. "You are the author of your life. You can edit or change the script," says Dr. Deepak Chopra. "…as you let go of the need to arrange your life the universe brings abundance to you…" We must believe in ourselves and let go of negativity. Challenges in life are not destroy us, but to uncover hidden potential and power. Visualise your body, mind and soul working together. Good times are ahead. Let go of all the things we cannot control and move forward with gratitude and abundance. When you can't control what's happening, challenge yourself to control the way you respond to what's happening. That is where your power is in order to build presence and make a statement or assert yourself, or just let people know who you are without being arrogant, boisterous, loud, and so on. This is also quite lame. In today's world, more and more people realize that such behaviour doesn't carry you forward for too long. It does not last. You can't sustain it for too long. So, unless I do something about my situation, who else can. It is only I who can do something about them. Therefore, let me try and take control of myself, my thoughts and my actions to build that presence. Let go of nervousness, let go of fear, let go of things that we clutch on to, thinking that we need power. Those who crave power will lose it ultimately. That goes for any material thing. The more you give, the more it comes back to you, giving to the universe and how the universe brings it back to you. So that is just beautiful. As you let go of the need to arrange your life universe brings abundant good to you. We need to do what we need to do, and then leave it to the universe to bring back the benefits for ourselves.

SIX AREAS TO ENHANCE PRESENCE

Coming back to presence. According to an article in the Forbes® magazine about Presence, there are six areas that are necessary to consider enhancing presence. At an overall standpoint, it says first, you have got to read the culture of the place, organisation or environment that you are dealing with. Understand the culture first. Who stands out in your company? Why? Who commands attention in a positive way? Look around for people to emulate. Seek out early and let go of the negative attention seekers. These could be the people who might actually be loud and distracting, trying to grab attention, and so on. Be careful not to emulate those people who really can't sustain their relationship. You will know them when you see them. Be careful about who you want to emulate and who commands attention in that positive way such that you can emulate such a person. So, first is to beat the culture.

Next, let's go down into a bit of detail read the room. To read the culture, you have looked at the overall environment and their context. Now, we are narrowing down to the room. Ensure that the way you carry yourself from dress to interaction aligns with the vibe and the needs of the room, the specific area or scope of activity. Conform to the overall code, way of dressing and style, so that you are seen as 'one among us', and make sure that we also understand those unwritten rules of interaction. Not everything is written and handed down to us. When you join a new organization, not everything is written down and therefore the first few weeks would be spent in observing what works here. How do people move around? How do they interact? How do they respond to each other, and so on and pick up the right signals and follow them so that there are things that we need to adapt. That is just a way by which you become a part of the pack and not left out or not seen as an outsider anymore. Many are able to do that really quick. All of us as professionals need to be able to gel in quite fast. That's the mark of a professional who has presence. Sometimes it might be a good idea to be a wee bit understated or subtle to be able to slip in and then begin to perform begin to be able to be part of the group getting noticed and so on. Some people tend to overdo it, get popular too quickly and it all comes crashing down, they become loners and miss the acceptance of the group. Do not overdo the need for attention or the need to be able to be recognized and so on. It will come about in its own time. Just do what needs to be done. So go micro read the room.

Third is you are in the room now, so read the people. Listen carefully. Listen without filters. Listen to what is being said and what is not being said. The chief quality or a skill amongst interpersonal skills is listening. In my book, it is the most important skill. It helps you read the culture and read the room and build relationships from there. Too often we are obsessed with our own anxiety of wanting to gain presence and attention that we miss listening to the others. At the end of the chapter, we have a call to action with a listening exercise.

Now you have read the culture, the room and the people. The only thing left is to read yourself. Be self-aware. Remember the career exercise that we did in Chapter Two? What strengths do you bring to the table? What is your reputation? What are your development areas? If somebody were to talk about you, what would they talk about? What is the feedback that you have got? Take feedback, be clear about the values, strengths and skills that you bring to the table. You can clarify all of these for yourself through specific exercises in the previous chapters. It is important for you to know everything externally. And it is important for you to know about yourself as well. What are you good at? What do others say you are good at?

Pay attention to the tone when you speak. At number five, a tone of confidence is critical. Eliminate disclaimers, the various breaks, which occur within the flow of otherwise fluent speech. These include "false starts", "fillers", such as "huh", "uh", "um", "well", "so", "like", and "hmm"; and "repaired" utterances, where speakers correct their own slips of the tongue or mispronunciations. They occur regularly in everyday conversation, sometimes representing upwards of 20% of "words" in conversation. Fillers might also be used as a pause for thought ("I arrived at, um—3 o'clock"), and when used in this function are called hesitation markers or planners. Working on eliminating these fillers brings about a tone of confidence. In addition, admit that you don't know, be vulnerable, have a confident humility. The I-know-it-all behaviour cannot be sustained for too long. If you have it, be aware of it and be mindful about its impact and tone it down. Next, calibrate yourself, if you're a reclusive introvert, like how I used to be, break out of your shell, begin to poke the shell from inside and look at which cracks you can make through, which ones will allow you to emerge out of and bloom. Find opportunities to break out of the shell, but take it slow, learning all the way, absorbing your body reactions to it and others acceptance of the changes you are making. If you're a garrulous extrovert, tending to be all over the place kind of a person tone it down. Be mindful of how you come across. Not to be self-conscious all the time, but self-aware. Build on your strengths and add a few quick wins here and there. It is okay to be an introvert and modify yourself as the situation comes up. It is okay to be an extrovert and modify your approach according to the situation. If you think you are an introvert, slowly begin to come out of that comfort zone by gently tugging at the natural boundaries. Do not make a whole lot of changes drastically overnight. It looks and feels awkward and might even slow down progress with negative effects. But make small changes, small tweaks to your persona, and you are going to be able to figure it out over a period of time. Take feedback, read the room, that's an art.

Supporting your presence is appropriate body language. Simple techniques would be to stand up straight, avoid slouching, be relaxed, appear open and undefended and practise open gestures. Open gestures always help. Keep a straight spine while sitting. Keep your feet hip-width apart and balanced. Breathe deep to the point just below your belly. Watch the other person's posture and mirror-match. That is exactly what I do when I'm in a room full of people – you smile at them from left to right at everybody, and you see most of them smiling back at you, nodding in your direction or acknowledging your presence, when you look back at them from right to left, mirror match the other person's posture. Stand still and avoid swaying on your feet. Smile as you walk into the room and smile when you're talking on the phone. You are seen audibly when you smile whilst talking on the phone and this conveys a lot of personality. Offer a firm but gentle handshake, knuckles, elbow or namaste as is accepted for the times and the culture. Maintain eye contact while connecting hands. Smile while greeting someone new. Avoid using the wall or large objects to prop you up - it conveys weakness. These are body language essentials from a physical standpoint that support building presence.

Exhibiting executive presence needs to be cultivated. Proceed step by step with each of the six areas to build your executive presence, your personality, your professional presence, and so on. Examine one area that you feel you need to improve amongst the six areas of presence listed here. Reflect on it. Share your area of improvement or concern with someone who you can ask for support and feedback. How do you plan to do that? Share your experience with how you have dealt with that area so far and what you have discovered about yourself. What has impacted you so far?

Remember, the other side of problems is challenges and opportunities. I recall an opportunity that came by to facilitate coach training sessions in countries across

Asia Pacific when I was still a young HR Manager. The opportunity was initially presented to me as a development program for me. If I were to let go of it for any reason another would get the opportunity. The thought of meeting people from many different nationalities initially terrified me. But I (physically) said yes, though my mind was still frozen. Taking the plunge early, working against my introvert-type fears and pushing myself to overcome the challenges made all the difference for years to come later. Considering these challenges and accepting them and being able to look at them as opportunities is a great way to progress. We are faced with uncertainty all the time. The world of work is always uncertain however along with it, there is always opportunity if you look for it. Act upon it when it happens. Do not fear trying out new things. You never know where your career will take you or where your ambitions will take you. If you try, you might win. Or you might lose. You have at least learned something. Therefore, always be shameless and fearless to learn, keep your mind open to the bigger picture. What have you identified for yourself to improve, to enhance your presence? Make sure that you build an action plan.

SUMMARY

- Read the culture of the place!

- Read the room.

- Read the people.

- Read yourself.

- Pay attention to the tone when you speak.

- Calibrate yourself - reclusive introverts, crack the shell, garrulous extroverts, tone it down.

- 'A quiet confidence is the best'.

- Repeat beneficial behaviours through your experiences to make habits.

- 'You are the author of your life. You can edit or change the script'.

- 'Our bodies, change our minds, and our minds change our behaviour, and our behaviour changes our outcomes.'

CALL TO ACTION

1. Try this V-sign exercise: Stand up wherever you are, use a cabin or a washroom with a mirror, and raise your arms above your head in a victory stance. Hold that posture for a minute while stretching slightly, observing yourself. Take a couple of long breaths and look at yourself in the mirror, doing the victory stance. How do you feel right now?

2. Here is a Listening Exercise. This is a test of listening focus and building higher self-awareness: Listen continuously for 10 minutes to a close family member - partner, child, sibling or someone really close to you - without your mind wandering. In case your mind wanders, bring it back to the listening. And count the number of times your mind wandered – record the number each time you repeat the exercise. Give your close friend feedback as to how many times your mind

wandered. If you cannot do the exercise in person, you can do it over a phone call, however it is better in person because you have body language, eye contact and a lot of things to work with. You might ask, what if the other person doesn't talk or they might just trail off or they may just stop. Start a conversation initially, to get the other person talking about something, you may or may not want to tell that person that you are doing an exercise but that is a call you can take. Try to keep it natural as much as you can, starting on the conversation and eventually ceasing to talk and continuing to listen for 10 minutes continuously. Then commence watching your mind and the steps that are described above.

"When we are able to take our focus off our anxieties, we are more likely to feel powerful."

"Presence is the state of being attuned to and able to comfortably express our true thoughts, feelings, values, and potential."

– Amy Cuddy

CHAPTER

06

Listening

*Listening is an art that requires attention over talent,
spirit over ego, others over self.*

– Dean Jackson

To understand what makes leaders role models in leadership, we need to understand key characteristics that set them apart. We discussed a few in the previous chapters. Each chapter builds on the earlier chapters referring to concepts, skills and techniques discussed or practiced. Leaders take their inter-personal skills seriously. They not only build on their presence in meetings but also make sure they listen completely to everything that is being spoken in a meeting; they seldom miss a co-participant's side of the discussion. Leaders may display introversion or extraversion. Irrespective of their type, their presence is not always defined by the garrulous extrovert who usually hogs the meeting making their presence known. People gravitate to where most of the noise comes from and in the process ignore the ones who are naturally quiet. "Listening is not a skill," says Peter Drucker, "it is a discipline." He also says, "The most important thing in communication is to hear what is not being said." Al Ritter sums it up beautifully, "Your listening, not your speaking, is your most direct access to leadership effectiveness."

Let us examine the exercise you took away to do in the last chapter – the listening exercise. What insights have you from this exercise? How many times did your mind wander? Two? Three? Five? Seven? Now, if your mind wandered, or even if it did not wander, what did you discover about yourself during that activity? What insights did you get about your style of listening? What else did you find out about yourself, especially when your mind wandered? And when you brought it back to listening, what happened? What did you think during the activity and after the activity? Was it consistent with your thoughts before starting the activity?

Some say they realise they can find interest in any conversation and listen with focus, without getting distracted; others miss their concentration and focus halfway through the conversation; some are very mindful and display behaviours such as patience and concentration irrespective of speaker or topic. One client said, 'focusing on listening to another can connect you emotionally'. Another says the one who is talking and listening, whether being listened to or not, opens up more when listened to completely. Yet another says my concentration depends on the topic and also the person I am. Eye contact in a conversation helps to show the person that you are interested in what they're saying, says a training participant. Another says that your tone matters. While someone else says, once you pull your mind back from wandering you are able to concentrate better. One client said, 'When I was off-track, I reminded myself to focus on listening; and by listening carefully I could actually get a lot deeper in my concentration.

All of this is true. The reality is different for different people. However, listening without judgment can get the speaker to speak to you more about the topic.

Clearing our minds of other thoughts and putting ourselves in the speaker's situation helps the focus. Focus in listening for many could depend on topic and also the speaker. When we listen without judgment, we can get the speaker to speak to more and it helps the conversation flow. These are discoveries of sorts. Given a chance to be listened to, most people are encouraged to keep a conversation going. What is the opportunity you are granting a speaker? The opportunity you are giving the other is the gift of listening. And you can embellish this gift further by choosing to let go of judgment. To do that during a conversation, the listener needs to bring back their attention to listening when they notice their mind wandering. When you bring your mind back from wandering, you find that you are able to focus better on listening. On the other hand, when you go off-track, you remind yourself to focus on listening back again and in doing this you gain more focused listening. You become more self-aware because you focused on the exercise intentionally.

If you did this exercise, what was going on in your mind? The exercise was to listen as well as count how many times your mind wandered. I hear interesting insights from folks in my group facilitation programmes. Many who did this exercise with their partner or spouse say that they experienced something very different that they feel they had ignored and thrown away for years of living together! They say they probably 'listened with focus' more during their romantic courtship days - and eventually ceased to be good listeners. As time passes, family relationships become very close bonds that we take for granted to different levels. Focused listening can become a casualty. Older folks admit how they have forgotten to listen over time. Many discover through this exercise that they are not really the good listeners they thought they were. It shows up at work as well. Years of baggage have eroded their ability to listen to connect.

TO IMPROVE YOUR LISTENING SKILLS TO A VERY HIGH DEGREE

Zig Ziglar once said, "Speak in such a way that others love to listen to you; listen in such a way that others love to speak to you."

If you intend to improve your listening skills to a high degree, there are two things you need to do: your objective must be: (a) to listen to what is being said, (b) understand what is being said, and (c) to possibly respond. To reach the first stage, there is an intermediate step, which is to focus the mind since the mind begins to wander. Remember, we are only talking about improving our listening skill. We are not focused on a specific individual or the current topic. The practice ideally must be done in the most 'difficult-to-listen topics', with the most 'difficult-to-listen-to person', or with someone you are very used to, you take for granted - that is a real test of your listening - because your mind will still wander. Bring back your mind to the listening. Continue to focus. This phenomenon keeps repeating until focus develops over time and diversions reduce. Remember what Amy Cuddy said? "Our bodies change our minds, and our minds change our behaviours, and our behaviours change our outcomes." Bringing back your mind to listening is a deliberate body action. This deliberate action changes the mind. The mind changes the behaviour, and you begin to focus with associated body language that represent your focused mind. 'Listening to connect' can thus improve with practice over time.

To get to the third stage that we described above in (c) which is to respond, the intermediate step (b) is to make sure that the mind is focused on what the person is saying. If the mind wanders, which it likely will, bring it back to the listening. Initially when you start doing this, it will be awkward, and you will find that in bringing the mind back you are listening a little awkwardly. In course of time, that awkwardness will give way to a habit. As you slowly keep doing it, you are being conscious, and if you continue to keep doing the action it becomes unconscious competence in course of time.

CONSCIOUS - UNCONSCIOUS COMPETENCE IN LISTENING

How do you make focused listening your unconscious competence? We can understand the entire cycle of learning focused listening through the four stages of competence model. The four stages of competence were created by Noel Burch in the 1970s as a model for learning. The theory behind it was initially founded by Martin M. Broadwell back in 1969. Remember the day you learned to drive a car. When you were a child, you would see cars zipping past and you would not know what it takes to drive one. You even do not know that you do not know. This stage is called the 'Unconscious Incompetence' stage. By the time you are eligible to gain a license to drive, you start learning with a teacher. You realise how much you do not know and how much there is to learn. This stage is called 'Conscious Incompetence'. Your unconscious incompetence gives way to conscious incompetence - and as you keep learning and practicing there is some awkwardness, but over time, and with overcoming the initial stumbling blocks you consciously gain a certain level of competence. You can drive with more ease and practice. You are much more comfortable now than ever before. You are in a 'Conscious Competence' state. As the years pass and driving is an everyday activity, you do not realise the sequential actions that you take to drive a car – the functions of driving are second nature, and they happen quite unconsciously. You go from point A to point B, and everything in between keeps happening automatically: you think about the day or the tasks that lie ahead, driving happens consciously but its constituent functions happen quite unconsciously. We say that you have now arrived in an 'Unconscious Competence' space.

The same it is with improving listening focus. The initial awkwardness of noticing and counting the number of diversions as well as trying to minimize them all fall within these stages – just like learning any new skill or technique. Ultimately, what helps with listening focus is watching our mind and making sure that the mind is brought back to listening when it begins to wander.

In training to become a certified coach I have undergone extensive practice in focused listening. What I thought was good listening before taking the course, was indeed not as much listening at all. With guidance, it is possible to become more self-aware of your listening focus, but it takes years of effort to make it a habit and maintain consistency of the listening practice. A full day of coaching sessions which deploys a high-level listening focus is likely to be far more energy-consuming than teaching or facilitating a full day of class. That is the amount of effort it takes for listening. Coaches need to completely listen to everything that is being said, to be able to repeat what the 'coachee' said, as well as hear anything that is not being said as well. This triggers questions further to clarify in order to move the client forward.

'NINE OUT OF TEN CONVERSATIONS FAIL TO MAKE THE MARK'

Well-performing managers are people who may have a very high quality of listening. They remember information and seldom miss data-points. It is said by Dr. Judith Glaser, the late scientist, researcher and author of the book *Conversational Intelligence: How Great Leaders Build Trust and Get Extraordinary Results*, that "nine out of ten conversations fail to make the mark". This finding is based on research over a 35-year period across thousands of conversations in organisations worldwide. Nine out of ten conversations fail to make the mark because people walked away with less than 50% of the understanding of what was spoken. People interrupting each other assuming they know the direction of the conversation or switching off halfway through listening because they do not like the direction the conversation is taking, all lead to a situation of understanding half of what was said. On the speaker's part we might hear them say, "Let me complete what I am saying…" or "wait till I finish…" and this is because people tend to put the critical parts of their message towards the end of what they are saying. It is therefore important to wait until the other person has finished speaking, even before beginning to prepare your reply. In other words, wait until the other person has finished speaking, before you begin to process your reply. Listening therefore does not happen with two stages – listening and responding – but with three stages: listen first completely until the other person has finished speaking; process your reply; and then reply. It is not going to take much longer than usual. It all happens in nanoseconds. All you need to do is to focus on developing the skill of 'listening to connect'. Leaders who have picked up this skill and have finetuned their listening find it easier to collaborate and perform.

SUMMARY

- Intentionality helps.

- Leaders listen completely.

- Be clear, concise and complete.

- Be mindful of your mind getting diverted.

- Certain key characteristics set key leaders apart.

- Clearing mind and getting into the speaker's shoes helps

- If the mind wanders, which it likely will, bring it back to the listening.

- 'Your listening, not your speaking, is your most direct access to leadership effectiveness.'

- In internal listening, you are listening to your own thoughts.

- In focused listening you have stopped listening to your own thoughts and you are completely listening to what the other person is saying.

- In global listening, you are putting yourself in the shoes of the other person and feeling what they are feeling as well.

CALL TO ACTION

Listen to Connect in three stages:

1. Listen completely until the other person has finished speaking.

2. Process your reply.

3. Reply

Watch your mind, to perfect 'Listening to Connect':

1. Listen for ten minutes to your spouse, partner or a close family member without your mind wandering.

2. If your mind wanders, bring it back to the listening.

3. Count how many times your mind wandered and write it down.

4. Observe if you can lower the number of times your mind wandered.

> *"To get to the next level of greatness depends on the quality of the culture, which depends on the quality of relationships, which depends on the quality of conversations. Everything happens through conversations. And the quality of the conversation depends on the quality of listening."*
>
> *– Dr. Judith E. Glaser*

07

Coaching

"Opportunities don't happen, you create them."

– Chris Grosser

Leaders need coaches and coaching is for all. Your career can develop manifold if you have a coach to support your leadership development. Often, I see executives accepting coaching only if it is sponsored by the organisation. Choose your way, but coaching, sponsored or not, can make the difference between a good leader and a great leader.

High-quality, effective leadership requires coaching as its key development component. Explore the question: "What's in it for me?" is important to understand how coaching results in long term benefits.

Coaching helps with specific business challenges which often require research and data collection. You can leverage data to confirm that your leadership coaching investment will address the issues on hand.

A case study revealed that leadership coaching helps leaders improve interpersonal skills, time management and prioritization skills, and helps them identify way to apply these skills at work. The following were the survey findings:

173% improvement in communication skills

83% improvement in time managerial skills

62% improvement in conflict resolution skills.

71% improvement in executive presence skills.

49% improvement in strategic thinking skills.

WHAT MATTERS TO THE LEADERS' STAKEHOLDERS

Diligently understand your stakeholders and analyse them. Who are your allies and your detractors? Use a stakeholder matrix to document how you will engage both of these groups. How can you demonstrate value for their functions or roles if you get into a leadership coaching program?

To engage stakeholders in other functions, ask questions and understand their challenges. Demonstrate how leadership coaching will solve their pain points as well. Find an influential senior colleague to be your program champion. This person should understand the benefits of a leadership coaching program, and ideally have seen these benefits first hand.

Work with stakeholders to understand what positive impact or ROI looks like. Identify key measures or evidence stakeholders would look for to demonstrate that leadership coaching has been effective. If there are any doubts, work with stakeholders to clarify them. Persuade them to work with you to run a pilot. This may seem like a small-scale approach, but once you have at least one story or case to illustrate impact, you can spread that story, and use it to move to the next stage of coaching for the organisation.

BE OPEN

Lack of trust make stakeholders sceptical of not only buying into a new leadership coaching program but contributing to it. If they feel there are any disconnects between the program manager, deliverables, success metrics, or program partner, trust may be an issue.

To mitigate trust issues, be transparent about any real or potential challenges, and solicit key stakeholders' feedback. Objectively offer a leadership coaching solution that you can deliver. Stakeholders trust more if you tell them the truth — even when the answers aren't perfect.

SET AND MEASURE COACHING GOALS

Establish clear, measurable goals for your leadership coaching program.

Metrics let stakeholders quickly assess value and progress. Think high level. Avoid getting into the weeds, as stakeholders likely won't have the time or inclination to process extremely detailed information. Further, focus on metrics that show business impact as quickly as possible.

Metrics are as important as the goals they are set to achieve. They help stakeholders understand what a leadership coaching program can accomplish. So, focus on the right goals. Once you set the goals, define the metrics, quantitative and/or qualitative measures that are easily digestible for all stakeholders.

ENSURE STAKEHOLDERS UNDERSTAND THEIR ROLE

At the end of the day, you should know the demands and motivations for key stakeholders, and they should trust you because you've been open and honest with them about the benefits and potential challenges associated with a high-quality leadership coaching program. They should understand the importance of their individual contributions to the program's deliverables and success, along with the benefits they can offer. After which, success will produce a tangible reward.

Clarifying these key items should engender the desired buy in and collaboration for a shared win, business gains, and a leadership coaching program you can use to amplify and build leaders across the organization.

CONVERSATIONAL INTELLIGENCE®

The CreatingWE® Institute launched the Conversational Intelligence® for Coaches 2016 program which I was privileged to be a part of. Conversational Intelligence (C-IQ) is a concept developed by Judith E. Glaser that explores the science and art of conversations.

It refers to the ability to "connect, navigate and grow" with others through the quality of conversations. Conversational Intelligence focuses on how the way we communicate influences relationships, trust, and the overall effectiveness of interactions within organizations and personal lives according to Judith Glaser.

KEY ASPECTS OF CONVERSATIONAL INTELLIGENCE®

Building Trust - Conversations build trust or erode it. High-quality conversations foster trust, while poor conversations can damage it. Trust is the foundation for collaboration, innovation, and effective teamwork.

The Neurochemistry of Conversations - Glaser emphasizes that different types of conversations trigger different neurochemical responses in the brain. For instance, open and positive conversations can increase oxytocin levels, fostering connection and trust, while defensive or negative conversations may increase cortisol levels, leading to stress and fear.

Levels of Conversation - Glaser categorizes conversations into three levels:

Level I: Transactional Conversations – These are focused on exchanging information and confirming understanding.

Level II: Positional Conversations – These conversations involve advocacy and inquiry, often leading to debates or discussions where parties aim to influence each other.

Level III: Transformational Conversations – These conversations aim to co-create, share, and discover new possibilities together, leading to deep understanding and trust.

The Importance of Listening - Effective conversations require active listening, which goes beyond just hearing words. It involves understanding the underlying emotions, intentions, and meanings behind what is being said.

Shifting from "I-Centric" to "We-Centric" - Conversational Intelligence encourages a shift from individualistic, self-focused conversations to more collaborative and inclusive dialogues where mutual understanding and shared goals are prioritized. Judith uses an interesting word, "co-creation" that is quite common amongst leaders today. It refers to the ability to 'create with' stakeholders rather than 'create for' stakeholders.

Creating a Conversational Culture - Organizations that cultivate a culture of open, honest, and constructive conversations can enhance leadership effectiveness, employee engagement, and organizational performance.

By improving Conversational Intelligence, individuals and organizations can create more effective, meaningful, and productive interactions, leading to better outcomes in both personal and professional contexts.

There are Conversational Essentials that can be followed by leaders and their teams to build trust networks as follows:

BEING OPEN TO INFLUENCE:

Judith says that this Essential is the overarching mindset and attitude that is cultivated to utilize the other essentials in a masterful and consistent way. As a leader we must cultivate an open mindset within ourselves, and when leading others we aspire to cultivate openness in them as well. With this mindset we embody curiosity. We are open to deeply hearing what others say without filtering it through our own agendas. We let go of being right and find the most powerful answers and insights in the process of connecting, cocreating and synthesizing ideas. We ask questions for which we have no answers, we encourage expression without expectation, and we enable a neutral mindset so we can hear what others are saying or thinking.

LISTENING TO CONNECT

This Essential is the overarching *internal action*, that we practice in all moments of leader type of conversations.

Listening to Connect – not judge, confirm or reject, is a way of listening to the other person with a focus on them, not you.

It's bigger than listening to understand – which is more about listening to confirm what you know. Listening to connect is about focusing your attention on the other person: What are they trying to say? What are they thinking? What are they hoping you will help them explore? Connect to their 'world' and explore their world.

ASK QUESTIONS FOR WHICH YOU HAVE NO ANSWERS.

Think of "Asking Questions for Which You Have No Answers" as the *external action* and overarching framework. Too often we ask questions to guide people to where we want them to go. That is felt by others as leading questions and can be interpreted as manipulation, putting people on guard, and activating our distrust networks. When we ask questions for which we have no answers, we are in a mindset of discovery and others feel this as inquisitive and curious. This puts people into a co-creating, trusting, and receptive state of mind. Asking Questions for which you have no answers opens and expands the conversational space for a whole new reality to emerge for you and others. This C-IQ essential activates a process of coregulation between you and your colleague – around 'discovery.' Together you create a space that activates new thought networks in the prefrontal cortex of you and your colleagues.

CONVERSATIONAL AGILITY

Conversational Agility is what we aspire to activate and create mastery in ourselves, through the use of all the Essentials and Tools. If Priming for Trust is the Foundation of the Essentials - then Conversational Agility is the roof over the house that all the Essentials built.

As Leaders it is our mission to assist others in becoming Conversationally Agile. In doing so we become mindful of our own conversational agility and mindfully focus on becoming role models. Without Conversational Agility one cannot move into different types of conversations with ease and co-create in harmony. When a conflict is brewing, interrupting the pattern through the use of Reframe, Refocus and Redirect is a powerful way to build the Conversational Agility muscle. It enables people to open to new energy, insight and outlook for wisdom and insight to emerge. For example, when we look at the Conversational Dashboard, we want to move from Resistor to Experimentor and from Protecting to Partnering. Using your Conversational Intelligence skills, you can use reframing, refocusing, and redirecting. The 3 R's are the way you refocus your conversations to elevate the communication abilities of everyone involved. This can be used with the overarching frameworks of Double-clicking and Asking Questions. As you master these skills you are helping yourselves to regulate your own neurochemistry and create a mind shift from your lower brain to your higher brain. When a company becomes adept at this, the whole company mindset-shift takes place, and the culture-change people will experience, is profound.

PRIMING FOR TRUST

Think of this Essential as the foundation of the Conversational Intelligence® house. Without actively priming for Trust no other essential or tool will be effective, and we can't build a solid house.

Be in constant reflection and co-creation of the following:

- How can I create a safe environment?

- Can I be more transparent about desired outcomes and share threats that may stand in the way?

- What actions, thoughts or words will enable the other person to shift from protect to partner? How can I establish rapport?

- How can I establish a 'power-with others' context?

- What actions, thoughts or words will enable us to listen to connect and relax judgment and ignite a sense of co-creation?

- What actions, thoughts or words will bridge between our realities?

- What can we say to reduce conflict and discuss what mutual success looks like?

- How can I approach my counterpart with caring, candour and courage?

- Can we identify Reality Gaps, and stay open to test assumptions?

- Can I/we stay in "Share and Discover" – listen to connect and be open to change our minds?

DOUBLE-CLICKING:

Double-Clicking is the Essential strategy. Double-clicking is a great way to ask questions for which you have no answers. It is actually a great strategy to use with all of the tools and a way to ask all of your questions. Asking "Why" or "What does that mean?" or "What else?" are very powerful yet basic double-click questions to insert repeatedly. Make these your best friend! As one double-clicks it reveals the deeper meanings held by oneself and others.

Through double-clicking we can better understand how we see the world and how others see the world. We gain clarity and understanding of what triggers us, but also gain understanding of others' perspective, their deeply held beliefs, and their points of view. By double-clicking, we make discoveries and personalize our own meaning. You as the leader are using the Double-Click C-IQ tool to activate the process of discovery thus increasing Conversational Agility. Sometimes people may say to you, "I don't have time to spend in deep conversations—they take too long." By utilizing all of the Conversational Essentials in tandem we can build Conversational Agility. Double-clicking, according to research, is neuro-chemical alchemy. What normally could take months or even years can happen instantaneously. It enables deeper connections, both in thought and co-creation to surface quickly. It bypasses the time-consuming, painful and emotional processes that normally need to occur, in order to clear away blocks.

In conclusion, think of these Essentials as the overarching frameworks in C-IQ, with Priming for Trust as the Foundation and Conversational Agility as the roof over everything. Use these frameworks (C-IQ Essentials) in any conversation to help people up-regulate the chemistry for connecting, navigating and growing with you. The C-IQ Essentials are conversational practices that can 'reset' your neurochemistry for health and can activate the ability to co-create with others with ease. You will be able to down-regulate behaviours that activate cortisol, and up-regulate the behaviours that activate oxytocin – thereby moving yourself and your partner into a trusting, generative, and partnering state of mind.

When you and your counterpart are able to master your own self-regulatory and co-regulatory mechanisms, and neurochemistry, the most powerful and healthy 'interaction dynamics' that exist in human nature, will be available to you.

THE GROW MODEL IN COACHING

GROW stands for Goal – Reality – Options - Way Forward. The GROW Model is one of the most established and successful coaching models. Created by Sir John Whitmore and colleagues in the 1980s, it was popularized in Sir John's best-selling book, Coaching for Performance.

Step 1 of the GROW Model – What are your Goals?

- Identifies and clarifies the type of goal through an understanding of ultimate goals,

- performance goals and progress goals along the way

- Provides understanding of principal aims and aspirations.

- Clarifies the desired result from the session.

  Step 2 of the GROW Model – What is the Reality?

- Assesses the current situation in terms of the action taken so far.

- Clarifies the results and effects of previously taken actions.

- Provides understanding of internal obstacles and blocks currently preventing progression.

  Step 3 of the GROW Model – What are your Options?

- Identifies the possibilities and alternatives.

- Outlines and questions a variety of strategies for progression.

  Step 4 of the GROW Model – What Will you Do?

- Provides understanding of what has been learned and what can be changed to achieve the initial goals.

- Creates a summary and plan of action for implementation of the identified steps.

- Outlines possible future obstacles.

- Estimates the certainty of commitment to the agreed actions.

- Highlights how accountability and achievement of the goals will be ensured.

SAMPLE WORKSHEET 1

Observe this conversation and try to identify if the GROW approach is followed:

Executive: Sir, can I meet you for a couple of minutes, please?

Manager: Yes, how can I help?

Executive: I find that the new targets where customers are referred to the product sales team quite challenging sir.

Manager: What is the problem?

Executive: Nothing specific sir, I just feel I will not be able to achieve them.

Manager: Nonsense. You are a good performer. You will be able to refer lots of customers.

Executive: I somehow feel stressed sir.

Manager: Everyone gets stressed. Don't worry. You will get used to it. You will be fine.

Executive: Sir, some customers ask me difficult questions and I don't know what to say.

Manager: You're not supposed to say anything. That's the product sales team's job and they are qualified to speak to them. If you try to give customers advice when you're not qualified, you will be in big trouble.

Executive: That's what I tell them. But I can see that they don't want to be referred. It makes me feel a bit incapable and useless.

Manager: Come on, now. You've got to pull yourself together. We've got tough targets this month. I'm relying on you. You're one of my best workers. Now think positive and give it your best shot.

SAMPLE WORKSHEET 2

Now observe this conversation and try to identify if the GROW approach is followed. What is different from the previous conversation? Note your differences in the table provided below.

Executive: Boss, can I see you for a minute, please?

Manager: Yes, how can I help?

Executive: The new targets sir, where we refer customers to the Products Sales Team.

Manager: You sound concerned.

Executive: I just don't think I'll be able to achieve them.

Manager: I know they're challenging, but you sound quite worried about them.

Executive: I just feel stressed about them.

Manager: What is it about them that makes you feel stress?

Executive: Well, some of the customers start asking me really difficult questions and I just don't know what to say.

Manager: What kind of questions?

Executive: Oh, about products, services and situations are they ordered in and how quickly they can receive them… things like that.

Manager: And how do you answer such questions?

Executive: I tell them I'm not qualified to answer those questions, and they'll have to ask the VAP Adviser.

Manager: That's correct. All discussions like that have to be with the product sales team only. Do you know why?

Executive: Because if we gave them wrong advice and from an unqualified person, we will be in trouble.

Manager: That's right. So, what is it about the situation that makes you feel uncomfortable?

Executive: I don't know.

Manager: Think it through. Imagine I'm a customer now and we've just had the conversation you've described. Tell me how you feel.

Executive: Well… I feel a bit odd.

Manager: Why is that?

Executive: Well Sir, I think it is because I started this conversation about products. Customer asked me a technical question; and now I am telling him that I am not qualified. So, he must be thinking: "why did he start this conversation in the first place?"

Manager: All right, so if you give them the information, whether it's correct or not, you are breaking the company rules. And if you don't give them information, you feel a bit silly?

Executive: Yes Sir, that's it.

Manager: What do you think the result might be, if you thought of a response other than "I'm not qualified to give you that information?"

Executive: Like what Sir?

Manager: Let us think this through. What would you like to say?

Executive: I suppose something like "The product team is more qualified than I am to give that information", or "the Adviser knows more about this than I do"?

Manager: Ok, how about something that makes it sound even more helpful?

Executive: Hmm… how about, "To ensure you get precise and up to date information, I would like our Product Team to help with the answers to your questions?"

Manager: Good. That sounds helpful, but not evasive. How do you feel when you say that?

Executive: Much better Sir, I think it's a professional response.

Manager: Would you like to try it today, and let me know tonight how you are doing?

Executive: Yes, I will Sir. Thanks, Boss.

Manager: No, thank you. You thought about it all through yourself. All that I did was, to ask you a few questions.

What is different from the previous conversation? Note the differences in the table provided below.

1st conversation	2nd conversation

SUMMARY

- Leadership coaching helps leaders improve interpersonal skills.

- Be open.

- Set and measure coaching goals.

- Ensure stakeholders understand their role.

- Build trust.

- Transactional conversations focus on exchanging and confirming.

- Positional conversations involve advocacy and inquiry.

- Transformational conversations aim to co-create leading to trust.

- Shift from "I-centric" to "We-centric" approach

- Create a conversational culture

- Be open to influence

- Listen to connect, not to judge, confirm or reject.

- Ask questions for which you have no answers.

- Practice conversational agility

- Prime for trust

- Double-clicking to understand better, dive deeper

- Practice the GROW model for coaching conversations.

CALL TO ACTION

1. Practice Coaching and Conversational Intelligence in day-to-day life.

2. Listen to connect, not to judge, confirm or reject.

3. Ask questions for which you do not have answers.

4. Practice the GROW model for coaching conversations.

"The successful networkers I know, the ones receiving tons of referrals and feeling truly happy about themselves, continually put the other person's needs ahead of their own."

– Bob Burg

CHAPTER

08

Belonging

"When we listen and celebrate what is both common and different, we become a wiser, more inclusive, and better organisation."

– Pat Wadors

We have a custom of saying, "good morning" or "good evening" to people. I mentioned a coach colleague having a pleasant greeting like "hello, my dear sunflowers"! We have different greetings and wishes for the people we meet. These greetings can energise, inspire and motivate not just the greeted but the greeter as well. It is an instant oxytocin generator! However, have we internalised these greetings to the point of politeness? How often do we greet with the lingering moment to establish eye contact and attempt to genuinely mean a 'good morning' that is actually pleasant, healthy, fulfilling and energising? Do we stop to think about the effect of our acknowledgement of another's presence? Do we acknowledge others in the organization while passing them? What are those ingredients of Belonging that a Leader needs to know? How does a Leader ensure that this feeling of belonging pervades the team and every sphere of its activity? How does a Leader recognize when the sense of Belonging is missing or selectively ignored? How did the role models we discussed in the previous chapter themselves work with the sense of belonging with their stakeholders? What are our responsibilities as responsible corporate citizens?

When I was thinking about 'Belonging' and started writing this chapter, my thoughts went to Michael Jackson's song *'We are the World'*. This song is perhaps the best panacea for all time, exhorting us to heal the world and make it a better place. We witness many events worldwide that are in conflict with peaceful living. These incidents are not new to mankind. We see senseless acts of violence in our pages of history over the last many centuries. This is where the song gives us direction. It reminds us that we are the world, and we are the children, and we need to stand together to support the underprivileged or the marginalised sections of society. Everyone needs to feel they belong. Belonging triggers higher motivation and therefore higher levels of engagement.

We are discussing Belonging in the workplace and amongst stakeholders. There used to be a popular show on Netflix called *Queer Eye* with a bunch of lovely people, they always showed me what focus on 'belonging' can do. The program celebrates the special skills of different people who together make a difference in the lives of others, otherwise forgotten and unsung heroes. We are drawing lessons from this popular program in celebrating diversity, inclusion, and belonging in this chapter as well looking at corporate social responsibility as a means of promoting diversity, inclusion and belonging. Let us look at a few aspects that make the world of belonging worth living.

Stepping into our current topic on Belonging, let us first examine a functional area called Corporate Social Responsibility that companies run to instil the community sense of belonging.

CORPORATE SOCIAL RESPONSIBILITY (CSR)

This is the name given to the function of a company's efforts to improve the society or community in which it operates. These efforts can range from donating to non-profits to doing their bit for implementing environmentally friendly practices. CSR is mandated under the law in many countries under a policy called the Corporate Social Responsibility policy. Companies generally need to report what they do under CSR in a year with the funds that are allocated to them. So, these companies have a separate function headed by a senior CSR professional.

So, you might be wondering why I have brought up the topic of CSR. CSR is an important mandated activity that fosters inclusion and promotes wellbeing. All areas of social responsibility fall under the purview of CSR. Here is the crux of CSR. If an organisation wants to promote CSR, they need to involve all sections of their employees. So how do they do that? One of the ways is to make sure that their values or principles have already integrated CSR. For instance, one of the values or principles could say that we do our bit for the environment or do our bit for the society or promote a greener or better ecosystem. Let us dive deeper into this idea of a better ecosystem. The ecosystem not only includes the material world around us but our fellow human beings as well. At this point, we have to bring up the ideas of diversity, inclusion and belonging. Let's take them one by one.

DIVERSITY

Diversity is everything that makes you and me unique. It could be in terms of skin colour, religion, caste, gender, mother tongue etc. According to Dr. J. Bernard Hsu, there are four different types of diversity: internal, external, organizational, and worldview - and one should aim to represent them all. Diversity in the workplace means that an organisation employs a diverse team of people who reflect the society in which it exists and operates. Diversity incorporates all the elements that make individuals unique from one another. So, diversity includes everything that makes you unique. A diverse workplace creates space and opportunities for more ideas and processes. Diversity of talent brings a broader range of skills among employees, as well as a diversity of experiences and perspectives which increases the potential for increased productivity. A diverse workforce is more likely to understand the customers' needs and come up with ideas to fulfil them. Diversity in the workplace will also increase employee morale and instil a desire to be more effective and work more efficiently. This will greatly increase the productivity of the business.

Leaders need to focus on bringing in diversity in the team. For reasons stated above, a diverse workforce further enhances a leader's capabilities and makes him or her even more effective. For a local or regional business to be diverse internally creates opportunities externally, because the talent that exists within pushes the boundaries of business potential. Are there any disadvantages of being too diverse? Well, one might want to spare a thought on some possibilities which if managed well can prevent any effects of too high a focus on diversity.

It is possible that with a mandate of increasing diversity, hiring managers can focus on leadership qualities too often as well as people who are over-qualified for some jobs. The nature of diversity ensures that you acquire experts from different cultures and geographies perhaps. Diversity can also create too many opinions because of the varied experiences in different contexts of the team members. For the same reasons, diversity in the workplace can reduce the amount of trust that exists. This is a typical problem in the storming stage of team development. Suddenly when an organization decides to make diversity a top priority there can be an immediate decrease in the amount of trust that is present in the workplace. This negative consequence impacts every population demographic even if people are from the same culture, educational background, and career experience. Some become hostile during an increase in diversity. Communication problems arise. Since diversity initiatives are usually left to a single person or function to implement, there is not a whole lot of support from the different functions and their team members. Complaints arise and usually the diversity initiative ends up in lip service.

Keith Miller, CEO and serial entrepreneur says that Diversity in the workplace 'requires a commitment from every level of the chain of command for it to be a successful experience'. If the CEO does not buy into the process or is half-hearted and pays lip service to the process, putting up appearances and not following through, then neither will the managers nor the team right down to the entry-level worker be engaged with the concept. 'We live in a society that expects instant results,' he goes on to say. Diversity can provide unique benefits, but provided adequate time is built in, to expect the revenue and productivity increases to arrive. Many initiatives are stopped before they can be successful either because of loss of interest, vision, or a pronounced lack of patience with the process.

The advantages and disadvantages of diversity in the workplace must be carefully managed for the results to be successful. It may be an evolutionary process that challenges everyone, but it is also an initiative that can help a company, and its teams thrive today, tomorrow, and well into the future.

INCLUSION

Inclusion is about creating a sense of fairness. It's about treating everybody in a fair and just manner. The Society for Human Resource Management defines inclusion separately from diversity as the achievement of a work environment where all individuals are treated fairly and respectfully. They have equal access to opportunities and resources and can contribute fully to the organisation's success. So, diversity and inclusion go hand-in-hand, but there is a subtle difference between the two.

The Institute for Community Inclusion says that Inclusion means that all people, regardless of their abilities, disabilities, or health care needs, have the right to be respected and appreciated as valuable members of their communities, participate in recreational activities in the neighbourhood, work at jobs in the community that pay a competitive wage and have careers that use their capacities to the fullest, attend general education classes with peers from preschool through college and continuing education.

An article titled Inclusion in the Corporate World, by Pieter Ligthart and Harsonal Sachar of Russell Reynolds Associates, says that despite spending significant funds and efforts to attract a diverse workforce, many companies struggle to grow and retain these employees. Having diverse talent alone is not enough. An inclusive environment that creates opportunities for all employees to realize their unique potential is critical to talent retention, they say. They tested this observation by surveying 2,167 senior executives around the world and asking them about their perceptions of diversity and inclusion within their current organization. They found that most companies 'struggle to define, measure and strategize for an inclusive culture', and there is much work to be done in creating truly inclusive organizations. They struggle to grasp "inclusion" in concrete terms. Nearly half of executives state that their organizations have a clear, holistic definition of diversity, while less than a quarter are aware of a definition of inclusion. It's not surprising then that executives indicate that their company is more likely to publicly align their business strategies with diversity than with inclusion. More of these interesting insights at https://www.russellreynolds.com/insights/thought-leadership/inclusion-in-the-corporate-world.

Pieter Ligthart and Harsonal Sachar also say that processes to measure inclusion, and systems to stay accountable towards achieving inclusion related goals are rare if not absent in corporate environments. Executives also indicate that companies tend to overestimate the importance of a diverse talent pipeline and underestimate the importance of an inclusive culture. Although more than half of companies (53 percent) prioritize the hiring of diverse talent, significantly fewer are focused on talent retention (47 percent). Further, only a quarter of companies are ultimately effective at talent attraction and retention, with 32 percent seeing diverse talent leaving due to a lack of inclusion, suggesting there are significant obstructions to creating an effective diversity and inclusion strategy.

Overall, companies struggle to articulate and measure inclusive cultures, and are largely uninformed about potential obstructions to effectively developing inclusive cultures. What can they do to improve? There are steps companies can take to create an inclusive culture. Diagnosing a company's level of inclusion to uncover gaps is a critical starting point. Inclusion Indices such as the one developed by Russell Reynolds Associates that allows CEOs and boards to quantify their organizations' levels of inclusion can be used. Surveys, train-the-trainer sessions, local workshops, all addressing the gaps can be run quite effectively with lasting results. Human Resources business partners play a significant role in getting local leadership engaged and involved with team workshops, empowering sub-leaders and engaging them in conversations about diversity and inclusion. Other actions include unconscious bias training, cross-cultural mentorship, assisted succession planning, and a host of other proven practices. The overall involvement of the leadership effectively translated to the management team and its team members addressing specific pain points and barriers to inclusion will be effective and self-sustaining in the long run.

BELONGING

Belonging is a human need. Do you remember the first time you stepped into a new place, be it a new house, a new educational facility, a new company? You would have been anxious and nervous. You would have questions about whether the people around you would accept you. Would they make you feel comfortable to ease the transition? How soon would you be integrated? Where would you fit? In your life, you would have seen some people do this naturally and with ease. Some take their time, and some tend to overdo it and find their place hastily. From the organisation's point of view or the team's point of view, if you see someone new joining, it's up to you to make that person feel comfortable and make them feel that they belong. So, the onus is on us to be able to do it for others. That's the whole point. Belonging is a need that is genetically wired in all of us. We all want to belong. And when we don't feel that we belong or are alienated, we do not function well in that kind of environment. So, it's about being able to make everybody feel that they are part of something. And that they are respected for who they are, their skillsets and their potential.

There are two sides when it comes to belonging. First is the light side; when a person feels that he or she belongs, they will be able to unlock their authentic self and learn more. Then there is the dark side; when people overdo and hastily try to fulfil the need to belong, they tend to compromise themselves. They will don a mask to become someone else to fit in. So, belonging is not just about fitting in but also about being authentic and being yourself. And that's precisely why all these three ideas of diversity, inclusion and belonging go together.

CSR AND DIVERSITY, INCLUSION AND BELONGING

One of the many policies that many companies have adopted as part of their CSR is diversity and inclusion. This is because of all that is happening in the world today; there is a significant focus on diversity and inclusion. In our companies, we might belong to different parts of the country; we might come from different cultures. Or there are only people of a particular race or a particular culture in an organisation. You might encounter situations of discrimination, either aimed at yourself or aimed at others. Unfair discrimination can happen anywhere, anytime.

We have to create that feeling of belonging for our new colleagues. I'll help you find your role in this activity. You can become a role model to belonging because you might be the beneficiary of this approach by someone else someday. Remember the lessons we learnt in the previous chapters? Extrapolate the learning you have taken away from those lessons to build on belonging. If an organisation promotes diversity and inclusion, the organisation needs to be diverse to show that we are all different, but we work together. We have come from different races, communities, states, cultures, and backgrounds, but we work together and promote diversity, inclusion and belonging. Such diversity would also mean we have diverse role models. Examples of these are gender or sexual orientation. You could have single moms and single dads. You have zonal cultures; you have language differences. You have differences in accent and language based on MTI or mother tongue influence. When someone speaks, you would be able to make out where that person hails from based on how he or she communicates. As an ambassador of the culture of belonging, your role here is to observe yet ignore these differences that set us apart. It does not matter. What should be of interest is what he or she has got to contribute to the team. When people are judged based on where they come from, or based on the culture they come from, or based on colour, community, religious orientation and symbols we tend to have a divergent team that struggles to align. However, as professionals of the future world, it is imperative to know that teams, where diversity and inclusion are highly regarded are the most productive teams. Such teams ignore issues of culture and race. They are built on respect and the capabilities of the team members. Everyone is treated with an equal opportunity approach on such teams. And that is what young professionals and leaders of the future need to imbibe early on.

YOUR PERSONAL CSR

Welcome every new member warmly. He or she is joining your team. Might not be your specific function, but they are still joining your team, the organisation. Now, if you work in a large multinational organization with 10,000 employees in one location, how could you do this? You could help newcomers orient themselves to the surroundings. You could ask them about their role and their function. Help them with any technical issues like keycards or lunch coupons. The point I am trying to make is this, if you know that there's somebody new around or somebody struggling with something, then it's up to you to make that person feel that they belong by offering support and making them feel comfortable.

This is where I return to the beginning of the chapter. When you greet someone new, don't do it out of politeness. Acknowledge their presence. Wait for them to respond to your greeting. Look them in the eye and mean it when you ask, "How are you doing?" People generally fling a 'hi how are you,' in your direction and walk off; without a lingering moment to get a response. So, genuineness and authenticity should accompany your acknowledgement, greeting and question. It's up to us to create that moment of belonging because we belong to the same team, the same organisation, and we have people coming in to contribute and support our efforts.

OPEN QUESTIONS STIMULATE BELONGING

We have to strive to make this part of our organisational culture. Showing that you care. Diversity, Inclusion and Belonging is not a training program - it's more like a way of life. For example, involve people in the meeting – don't just wait for them to contribute. Let us say, you have called a meeting with a few team members. Some of them are vocal with their input and some of them might just stay quiet. Let us say the meeting is called to take a collective decision. It is natural to divert your attention to the ones who talk and possibly ignore the minority that is quiet. It is up to the meeting leader to involve everyone. The leader could ask the team if everyone is okay with a decision he has proposed, saying "Is this decision, okay?" The most likely answer from the quieter people might be a 'Yes'. Because such a question gives only two possible answers, 'Yes or No', and 'Yes' is convenient. Leaders tend to ignore the quieter ones. This could be a matter of judgement, that the vocal ones have the answers, and the quieter ones do not. The best leaders are people who avoid judging the team as such, in these situations. They consider everybody around the table as capable of contributing. It's up to the leader to draw them out. The skill of involving is an interpersonal skill, just like listening and questioning. Instead of asking if they agree with the decision, they would ask them to share their insights and opinions. The difference lies in asking open questions and closed questions.

Closed questions will only result in a yes or no answer, most of the time. When you ask a closed question, you might be inadvertently imposing your hierarchical superiority to influence the team member to agree. Now leaders may actually use that approach exactly for that purpose. But when you ask for their opinions and insights with genuine interest, using open questions, you express a sense of respect to their knowledge and expertise. An open question would prompt them to come up with a descriptive answer. Such questions often start with 'what, where, why, when, and how,' and often with 'what'. In the coaching fraternity, we only use open questions because they open up the client to respond both descriptively and sans bias. A simple example of closed and open questions is, you might ask someone, "Did you have lunch today?" Or you could ask, "What did you have for lunch today?" The first question elicits a 'yes' or 'no' answer. The second question will provide you with several details. Open-ended questions bring inclusion. When you ask open questions, you involve people. You make them feel elevated. When one feels elevated, one's oxytocin levels go up and one feels motivated to contribute. That's what open questions do. And good leaders always do that to involve everybody around the table. Back to our example of the meeting, the best way to involve the quieter ones would be to ask them a 'what' question – say, "some feel that this is the direction to take, what do you think?"

Talking of inclusion from different geographies, in one of my workshop sessions, one of the participants mentioned the example of UBC game developers. The participant was interested in computer games, and one of his favourite games was made by UBC. He discovered that the team that developed the game was multicultural. He found that these diverse backgrounds were reproduced in their games in terms of their stories' cultural, demographic, geographical, and historical contexts.

Returning to *Queer Eye*, the lead characters in the show come across as a comprehensive group. But they bring to the table their specific individual capabilities. They consist of a chef, an interior designer, a fashion designer, a coach, and a hairdresser – all accomplished experts in their own fields. They are from different backgrounds. They have different orientations. They come together, and they want to help. That is the common cause that binds them. They ask people to nominate others whose lives could be improved. Then they set about doing it. One episode featured a widower and single father named Josh. Josh's community nominated him to be the beneficiary of the team's reality program as he was struggling to make ends meet and was under tremendous mental stress. Every episode is moving and is a tearjerker. They bring up a variety of subjects, and audiences and is high on the message of inclusivity. They help people who have been marginalised, who have been ignored, and left to fend for themselves. These cast were themselves marginalized at some point of time in the younger days, they know the pain of being left out and ignored and therefore focus on people to make them feel they are wanted. And you are well aware that many communities still do not recognise or take kindly to people with different orientations. So, they generally move into societies that accept them.

The people who participate in drag races are called drag queens. RuPaul in the Netflix show pictured in the pink suit transforms himself into a gorgeous drag queen. It's a skill that several drag queens have displayed successfully worldwide, where their capabilities have been recognised. RuPaul's Drag

Race is a reality cum competition show. So, the contestants get a theme and have to use materials and make-up from a storeroom. They have to a fashion show with those materials and the theme in question. Drag queens have been popular in the US and Europe for the last 20 years. Some of them have even become very successful in crafting big businesses. In more conservative societies, drag queens are still struggling to come up and make a mark for themselves.

There are several heroes amongst us who do their bit to make the society a better place than what they have experienced themselves. These are all examples of what is happening around us. I would invite you to take a look at these shows. These shows echo displays of diversity, inclusion and belonging practiced in safe environments.

One of the best ways to find that moment of belonging is to find commonalities. You can only do so when you know each other beyond work. And is there any better way to know someone more personally than the sharing experience mentioned above? When you share such experiences, you become relatable. You feel a sense of empathy. When you develop empathy, your bond with people evolves from a functional and transactional bond to a relationship. If you need any task to proceed smoothly, it is best to cultivate such bonds. Appreciate each other's struggle. And there are people amongst us who all of us have a story. We all come with a story. Remember the ice-berg model? The story exists beneath the surface. Knowing these stories and appreciating their strengths, courage, perseverance and integrity, make people feel comfortable by being respected and considered. Listening to their stories helps bring about bonds that never existed before. Share their delight when they talk of their triumph over adversities. "Diversity is being invited to the party; inclusion is being asked to dance," said Verna Myers.

CULTURAL DIVERSITY

Cultural Diversity can be a source of creativity, or it can be a source of team problems, such as miscommunication and lack of understanding. Therefore, leaders need to be culturally sensitive and apply flexible leadership within the team. The exercise you will do here is to write down something unique about your team members or the people around you. Find out where they come from, what their traditions are, their festivals, traditional dresses, types of food and so on. Avoid topics of political leaning or religious orientation. Focus on all the beautiful aspects of the cultures that your team members come from.

SUMMARY

- CSR is an important mandated activity that fosters inclusion and promotes wellbeing.

- Diversity is everything that makes you and me unique.

- Inclusion is about creating a sense of fairness.

- Belonging is a human need.

- help newcomers orient themselves to the surroundings.

- Open questions are involving questions stimulate belonging.

- One of the best ways to find that moment of belonging is to find commonalities.

CALL TO ACTION

If you want to be ambassadors of diversity, inclusion and belonging, it is vital to consider your experiences. The exercise is quite simple.

1. Write down in your notebook your most difficult or saddest moment. Then write down your happiest memory. After writing them down, please share what you have written with someone you know. Talk about your experiences and ask your listener to share their similar experiences with you. Recognise the feeling of sharing and the feeling when you hear someone else share.

2. After this conversation, write down the feelings you experienced during this conversation. How did they differ when you shared your difficult moment and your triumphant moment? What did you feel when someone else shared something from their life with you? Write how you will create and foster moments of belonging in your organisation or institution.

3. Imagine yourself as the CEO of a company. What steps would you take to improve belonging based on the information you have collected?

"An individual has not started living until he can rise above the narrow confines of his individualistic concerns to the broader concerns of all humanity."

– Martin Luther King, Jr

CHAPTER

09

Influencing

Never underestimate the influence you have on others.

– Laurie Buchanan

You can't influence people you refuse to associate with.

– Andy Stanley

You might know the song, *The Greatest*, by Sia. I love that song for a reason. The topic that we are going to discuss is *influencing*. It is about not giving up - and not giving up for a good reason.

"…Don't give up, I won't give up,

Don't give up, no no no

Don't give up, I won't give up.

Don't give up, no no no

I'm free to be the greatest, I'm alive,

I'm free to be the greatest here tonight, the greatest,

The greatest, the greatest alive

The greatest, the greatest alive…"

However, to influence for a win-win, I need to explain influencing to you from a professional and team point of view. It may not be the regular connotation of influence that we hear in day-to-day life. More on than that in just a bit. Let me take you to where we are on this journey. We are at the penultimate chapter in this book. Our objective is to engage, reflect, relate, connect and possibly find solutions to potential issues that will affect progress.

Let us stop for a moment and recall what we went through in the previous chapter. What does *'Belonging'* mean to you again? You might want to choose one or more options here:

i.   The product of being Diverse and Inclusive?

ii.   Accepting all types of unique people for who they are?

iii.   Diversity and Inclusion are a way of work-life?

iv.   Being Inclusive in our approach is being fair to all?

v.   Being able to ask, "How are you?" and mean it?

vi.   All the above?

vii.   None of the above?

What do you think?

Excellent! The correct answer is "All of the above." Each one of those options is important. They are all definitions or meanings of the word *'Belonging'* in the organisational context. Accepting all types of unique people for who they are; being able to ask, 'How are you?' and mean it; being inclusive in our approach, which is being fair to all - yes, diversity and inclusion is an ideal way of work-life, and the product of being diverse and inclusive supports performance.

What does *Belonging* really mean in a social and team context? The attitude towards Belonging as a typical team behaviour is becoming much more relevant now. It is the sort of glue that holds together the bonds of relationship, friendship, stakeholder-ship or plainly, a way of healthy work-life.

In the 2020-21 lockdown work-from-home situation, a lot was put to the test. I was delivering a 'lockdown' lecture remotely to an MBA school and its stakeholders worldwide, with about 2,000 people listening in. I was talking to them on the topic of "Belonging". There were a couple of questions from the audience. "How can companies and HR bring about better engagement especially during this (pandemic-lockdown) time?" and "How important is it to focus on engaging employees better?" The very fact that these questions were asked indicated that people who were working during the peak pandemic-lockdown, were experiencing uncomfortable situations at work, often by insensitive management or HR. In many organisations, there was a panic attack. Consequently, the way the HR or the bosses might treat employees could look dismal, like the sight of migrant-labour caravan trails at that time made us feel. Discarded. Ignored. Left to one's fate and pushed to perform unmindful of the risks involved. So, getting mistreated, losing jobs, losing pay, challenges in getting emergency medical aid for non-covid related ailments and so on were just some of the problematic effects of the pandemic induced lockdown.

Everybody had somebody who was going through tough times. Authorities were doing some things to alleviate the general suffering, but there was just too much of it going around. And this is the time one would expect HR and management to step in with empathy, rally their team members and make them feel that they belonged. HR needed to play the role of the mentor and healer. Some did. Many did not. There is a lot of heart that needs to go into dealing with people in this situation. One state decided to sensitise their citizens to the travails of migrant labourers who were far away from home and in despair. They started referring to them as *guest workers*. Migrant labour versus guest workers. What a change in perspective! And that is what I would say to my fellow HR colleagues and Managers. Be sensitive. It is crucial to deal with people and situations with extra empathy and gentle humaneness amid crises when everybody is under stress. Because, tomorrow, when the business is under economic stress, you would have a grateful team standing by you stoically and supporting your every need to survive. It is simply the right thing to do. Everybody wants some respite with the lockdown, and the situation still being pretty grim. Understanding is vital for *Belonging*. It is a way of life that needs to get ingrained into individual behaviour.

What then is Influencing? Why is it important? Is it a social process of interaction? Is it a process by which you want to achieve something without formal power? Is it a process by which people change their opinions or behaviour? Or is it a process to gain an undue advantage? What do you think?

Let us examine these questions:

It is a social process of interaction because you can only influence others by having a minimum level of interaction with them.

It is a process by which you want to achieve something without formal power because if you did already have control (read as 'power vested in a boss'), you would not need 'influencing skills'. However, it might help you influence upwards or others in your sphere of influence.

It is also a process by which people change their opinions of behaviour because that is the whole idea of influencing.

However, is it a process to gain an undue advantage? No. That is the difference between 'influencing' as referred to in a general, public context and influencing as referred to in the context of stakeholders. Here, we are discussing influencing the workspace, in the professional arena, in the corporate space, and with stakeholders - people who have an interest common to your interest. People can be defined as stakeholders when they are internal customers or internal suppliers and members of the same team or organisation. We are not talking about the routine day-to-day connotation of influencing that you hear about in the public domain. There, influencing is seen as a process possibly to gain an undue advantage. We are talking about influencing stakeholders within the organisation within the professional sphere. And in such a situation, it is definitely not a process to gain an undue advantage. We are talking about *influencing with integrity*. We are talking about influencing to arrive at a win-win situation for all the parties involved. We are focused on the skills and behaviours that lead to effective influencing.

In a TED Talk titled "What I learned from 100 days of rejection", Jia Jiang, a user of Jason Comely's Rejection Therapy, a website that provides inspiration, knowledge and products for people to overcome their fear of rejection, talks about how to handle rejection. His book, *Rejection Proof,* takes you on a journey past fear through rejection and empowered courage. One action that he advocates in his talk to handle rejection caught my attention. Embrace it. Embrace that feeling and let it fizzle away. The more you embrace that gnawing, negative feeling, the more it weakens and dies. Therefore, do not push it away because it will still come back to haunt you.

How comfortable are you to handle rejection?

Very comfortable?

Somewhat comfortable?

Somewhat uncomfortable? Or

Very uncomfortable?

Many of you might say 'somewhat uncomfortable'. That is reasonably expected. Rejection happens all the time. Some subtle and some pronounced. So, the one word that Jia Jiang uses to handle rejection, as he says, is to embrace it - and let it pass. If you push it away, the next time, the difficult feeling of being rejected will still come back to haunt you. You're always going to feel a little bad about it. Therefore, why push it away? When it keeps coming, the more you push it away, the more it comes back to haunt you. It is the same with the feeling of rejection, as with the feelings of anger, sadness, the feeling that follows after being let down, and the feeling of being defeated. There is that acrid and lousy feeling. So, what he says about rejection is also applicable to any negative emotion you're facing. Embrace it.

When you feel angry, instead of pushing it away, embrace that feeling. Embrace that rejection. Because when you embrace that, rejection becomes your friend. Until then, it's a nightmare. So, it keeps coming back. So, convert it to your friend, embrace rejection, and the more you embrace it, the more it would just fizzle away. So, do not be afraid of rejection. Embrace it. That is the one key strategy that is needed to understand how to deal with rejection. The more you can embrace rejection, the more it becomes a part of you. And the more you will calmly proceed to the next steps of influencing. Why is calm preferred? How will I get it?

"Our bodies change our minds, and our minds can change our behaviour, and our behaviour can change our outcomes," says Amy Cuddy in her book "Presence: Bringing Your Boldest Self to Your Biggest Challenges." Got the drift?

The Push-Pull Influencing Styles Assessment by David A. Schmittlein and Duncan Simester, professors at MIT Sloan School of Management is a great way to understand your influencing style. I want you to draw three columns. This is the scoring chart that you're going to use. There are 36 questions. For each of the questions, you need to put your choice in the right column.

The answers to the questions will be the numerals 4,3,2,1, and 0.

If you definitely agree with the question, the answer would be 4.

If you are inclined to agree with the question, then write down 3.

If you are undecided about the question, then your answer would be 2.

If you are inclined to disagree with the question, then write down 1.

If you definitely disagree with the question, the answer would be 0.

Another key issue to keep in mind is that while you consider these questions carefully, do it quickly. Only when you look to answer these questions quickly would you replicate your day-to-day behaviour. Be frank and enter the score of your choice. Let us return to the columns. The first column is the serial number. You can ignore the second column, but you need the third and the fourth. Therefore, you are using only three columns: serial number, Column A and Column B.

Okay, so here we go.

Column A	0-4	Column B	0-4
I often delegate important tasks to others, even when there is a risk that I will be personally criticised if they are not done well.		I put forward lots of ideas and plans	
I'm willing to be persuaded by others.		I usually put together good logical arguments.	
I encourage people to come up with their own solutions to problems.		When opposed, I'm usually quick to come forward to the counter-argument.	
I am usually receptive to the ideas and suggestions of others.		I often provide detailed plans to show how a task should be done.	
I am quick to admit my own mistakes.		I often suggest alternatives to proposals that others have made.	

I show sympathy towards others when they have difficulties.		I push my ideas vigorously.	
I listen carefully to the ideas of others and try to put them to use.		It is not unusual for me to stick my neck out with ideas and suggestions.	
If others became angry or upset, I tried to listen with understanding.		I express my ideas very clearly.	
I readily admit my lack of knowledge or expertise in some situations.		I defend my ideas energetically.	
I often put as much effort into developing the ideas of others as I do my own.		I often anticipate objections to my point of view to be ready with an answer.	
I often help others get a hearing.		I frequently disregard the ideas of others in favour of my own responses.	
I often listen sympathetically to people who do not share my views.		When other people disagree with my views, I do not give up. Instead, I tried to find another argument to pursue them.	
I am quite open about my hopes, fears and aspirations and my personal difficulties in achieving them.		I am imaginative in producing evidence to support my own proposals.	
I usually show tolerance and acceptance of other people's feelings.		I usually talk about my own ideas more than I listen to those of others.	
I usually accept criticism without being becoming defensive.		I present my ideas in a very organised way.	
I often help others express their views.		I think frequently draw attention to inconsistency in the ideas of others.	
I go out of my way to show understanding of the needs and wants of others.		It is not unusual for me to interrupt others while they are talking.	
I don't pretend to be confident when in fact, I feel uncertain.		I often put a lot of energy into our arguing about what to do.	

I want you to total the scores of both columns. Have the total score for Column A and Column B separately. Column A indicates a Pull style. Column B shows a Push style. For greater interpretation, if your score for any column is between 54 and 72, you definitely use that style. If your score is between 42 and 53, you have a tendency to use that style. And if your score is between 30 to 41, you are ambivalent about that style. However, if your score is between 18 to 29, then you tend to avoid that style. And if the score is between zero to 17, there's definite avoidance of this type.

Neither score is better than the other. It's just the way you are. We are not assigning any qualities like good or bad to either of these styles. You can be the pushy type or the pulling type. It is just about being effective. I have seen salespeople be successful based on the Push style. However, you should be wary if you score very high on the Push scale. You might rub people the wrong way, and they may resist you. For example, if I try to use a Push style as a salesman, I'll come across people who will stonewall me as they won't like the Push style. So, in this case, I'll have to step back. In fact, I'll have to step back quite early to see if the Push strategy is working or not. If I have a good score in the Pull scale, I can opt to use that strategy instead.

It is very rare to find people on the extreme ends of these scales. Personally, I'm more a Pull style of person than Push. But if needed, I can adapt to the Push style to get things done. I want to remind you once again; this questionnaire is just to find your natural style. So, when you use your natural style, look to see if it is working. If it's not working, take a step back and modify yourself and use the other style for which you might have a tendency. However, if your score is below 29 on either of the scales, it will not work for you. It will be a complete alien exercise, however much you try.

WHAT IS PUSH AND PULL STYLE?

The Push style is characterised by proposing and giving information. Overuse of it will end up with people blocking and shutting you out. The Pull style is characterised by testing, understanding, seeking information and building. No style is superior to the other. You just need to be self-aware and mindful about whom you're dealing with and look for early signs as to whether your style is working. We have talked about the limitations of overusing the Push style. If you overuse the Pull style, your niceties may stop working.

TOOLS OF INFLUENCING

There are seven tools of influencing. You have already gone through two tools. One tool is rules. In this scenario, you are the boss. You just dictate the process by stating that this is the rule and people have to follow. You don't need to do anything else but state the rule. The next tool is to express what you want and be silent. State what you want and avoid over-explanation. The next tool is based on logic. You start with the problem. Then you explain the best way forward. You could also ask others to contribute to the plan. If we are to recall the previous chapters, you do so by asking open-ended questions. You would be able to do so based on the relationships built on similar values. When you do so, you are already influencing. Now, in terms of stating what you want, I want to give you one particular tool that is very, very useful.

STATING WHAT YOU WANT

You might say this is easy. However, there is a way to state what you want clearly. The natural human tendency to convince someone about something is to make a statement and then explain why that statement was made. However, this is a wrong idea. You might be walking into a trap and fail to influence your stakeholder. Are you confused? Here is why. When you state what you want and then give reasons, you open up the space for debate and one-off tangential conversations. Such conversations distract from your central purpose of influencing your stakeholder. You need to be clear, concise and complete in your statement. So how do we go about this? Give the reason(s) first and then your statement, NOT the statement, and then a deluge of reasons. And after stating what you want, provide the silence.

For example, you say, "I want this", and then you explain why you want it; you have already weakened your position. And you are building up enough ammunition for the other person to say "no". Instead, give all your reasons why you want what you want. And then say, "…and for these reasons, I want this." And then provide the silence. Do not add anything but continue to provide eye contact. You have possibly left the other person expecting you to say more and give more reasons and justifications. Instead, remain silent, provide eye contact, and exude hope. This is when your position becomes very powerful because silence is powerful. Silence is uncomfortable for a lot of people. And that's why it can become a powerful tool for you. When you provide silence at that point, you come across as being conclusive. There is a sense of finality in the air. Let me give you an example.

Take the case of competitions like Master Chef Australia. After each round, when it is time to announce the winner, the judges line up all the contestants. They proceed first to eliminate the contestants who have not passed that round. How do they do this? Observe the next time closely. The judges say, "John, you came into this competition with a flourish, you had these successes, and you had these challenges. All of that was a great experience. However, in this particular competition, you're started well, but you made this mistake at this crucial moment, and <u>for this reason, you're going home</u>. Silence.

The decision sounds final. It is not up for debate. That is very clear. The technique naturally indicates that there is no room for argument and that the door is not left open. It is shut with that statement. Remember, reason – statement – silence.

Now repeat this five times:

Reason → Statement → Silence

Reason → Statement → Silence

Reason → Statement → Silence

Reason → Statement → Silence

Reason → Statement → Silence

CALL TO ACTION

I have two situations. In one situation, you have to influence your boss, and in the other, you have to influence a peer. Think of what styles you can use. Write it down in your notebook.

Influence is when you are not the one talking and yet your words fill the room; when you are absent and yet your presence is felt everywhere.

– Temitope Ibrahim

You don't have to be a 'person of influence' to be influential. In fact, the most influential people in my life are probably not even aware of the things they've taught me.

– Scott Adams

It is more important to influence people than to impress them.

– Adrian Rogers

CHAPTER

10

Courage

Do you have the courage to distribute decision-making power and ability in your organisation, or are you afraid your colleagues will prove to be at least as capable as you are? Do you have the courage to take time to reflect and try to find a smarter way, or are you afraid that will make you fall behind?

– Joakim Ahlström: 'How to Succeed with Continuous Improvement.'

Let us discuss courage for continuous improvement - a great way to end this book while you continue your journey. Rachel Platten's *Fight Song* that my daughter Neha introduced me to, sang and recorded once pretty is a reflection of my journey so far. This song has inspired her much as well. Read the lyrics here and take a listen when you can:

"Like a small boat

On the ocean

Sending big waves

Into motion

Like how a single word

Can make a heart open

I might only have one match

But I can make an explosion

And all those things I didn't say

Wrecking balls inside my brain

I will scream them loud tonight

Can you hear my voice this time?

This is my fight song

Take back my life song

Prove I'm alright song

My power's turned on

Starting right now, I'll be strong

I'll play my fight song

And I don't really care if nobody else believes

'Cause I've still got a lot of fight left in me

Losing friends and I'm chasing sleep

Everybody's worried about me

In too deep

Say I'm in too deep (in too deep)

And it's been two years I miss my home

But there's a fire burning in my bones

Still believe

Yeah, I still believe.

And all those things I didn't say

Wrecking balls inside my brain

I will scream them loud tonight

Can you hear my voice this time?

This is my fight song

Take back my life song…

A lot of fight left in me

Like a small boat

On the ocean

Sending big waves

Into motion

Like how a single word

Can make a heart open

I might only have one match

But I can make an explosion

This is my fight song

Take back my life song…

Know I've still got a lot of fight left in me."

Source: LyricFind

Songwriters: Dave Bassett / Rachel Platten

Fight Song lyrics © Sony/ATV Music Publishing LLC

Artist: Rachel Platten

Album: Fight Song

Released: 2014

Genre: Pop

To survive like life champions, we absolutely need the fight in our lives. And to survive life itself, we need our fight song. Everyone has a story. We all come with a story. Each one's story is unique and important to them. We can learn much from everyone's story.

The last discussion of this journey is about taking the courage to develop ourselves continuously. I want to leave you with some loud thinking points about taking courage. To echo the words from the song: "This is my fight song… Take back my life song… Prove I'm alright song… My power's turned on, starting right now I'll be strong, I'll play my fight song… And I don't really care if nobody else believes… 'cause I've still got a lot of fight left in me. This is a fight that makes me stronger to overcome challenges and invigorates me.

Those of you who know the song might love the song for its lyrics and how it is sung because it stimulates action; we need words of inspiration. We are not sure how long adverse conditions will last, but we are all in it together. We are there to support each other. There are platforms available for you to seek that support. Spare a thought for people who feel that they do not have that support. Some people have given up hope or lost hope altogether, those who feel the burden too heavy to carry on. You might see them around you as well. Fear, worry, and stress are normal responses to perceived or real threats, and at times, we are faced with uncertainty or the unknown. So, it is normal and understandable that people are experiencing fear in the context of uncertain and complex circumstances. There have been significant changes to our daily lives and with heightened focus on safety and unexplained situations we are left with. We have been faced with the new realities of working from home, temporary unemployment, home-schooling of children, and lack of physical contact with other family members, friends, and colleagues this decade. It is important that we look after our mental, as well as our physical health,' says the World Health Organisation. But much can be achieved if we stay focused on our objectives to engage, reflect, relate, bond, and resolve.

BRINGING IT ALL TOGETHER

Recall our discussions so far. The 'push' and 'pull' styles of influencing define the way you network. Leadership styles get deployed with Values. Our Presence is felt by the way we use these styles in our day to day lives. The push style for example is characterised by the use of such types of behaviour as Proposing, Giving Information and Blocking or Shutting Out. The Pull style is characterised by behaviours such as Testing Understanding, Seeking Information and Building consensus.

However, overuse of the push influence style can lead to blocking and shutting out. If a pushy salesperson tries to hard-sell something, one would stone-wall them expressing unwillingness to engage in the transaction. Therefore, overuse of the dominant push style can lead to a response such as blocking and shutting out.

The Pull style is characterised by testing understanding, seeking information, and building, so people who have a dominant pull style take the participative approach. This is not to say that the push influencers do not take the participative approach. The tendency is to tell, give information, propose and seek consensus, seek approval, or seek a sale.

While influencing, 'stating' is a technique that can be used to give your reasons for making the statement, then making your statement and following it up by silence. No points for guessing the right sequence: you need to give your reasons or explanation first, and then make your (clear, concise, and complete) statement, following up the statement with silence. Remember: making a statement and following it up with reasons is a natural approach we might take, especially if we focus on influencing quickly and carrying that stress on our minds. But doing it that way is a strict NO, which is why most people find themselves getting into an argument – you have left the door open for debate. And when you get into an argument, it could be inconclusive because it is not easy to win an argument. Therefore, the way to avoid an argument is to give your reasons first, make a statement and provide the silence. Avoid the trap of having to over-explain and over-justify your statement. That is a great way to influence. Be mindful and craft your influencing approach carefully. These are my key tips on influencing. There are, of course, several models to learn from on how to influence stakeholders for a win-win scenario, and influence with integrity but we could leave that for another book.

MAKE CHANGE A DESIRABLE COMPANION

Here are a few statements. Think about each statement and reflect on how it impacts you:

I am consistent.

I set my priorities.

I am open to development and change.

I am responsible for my own learning and development.

I learn and grow through a culture of constructive feedback.

I'm prepared to challenge set practices to drive innovation creatively and courageously.

Remember you are the author of your book; you can change the course if you want. Everybody is supposed to ensure that they can make a change and ensure that they are prepared for such a change. It's imperative to be sure that you're ready for change. It's crucial to accept change, and it's vital to know that change can happen at any point. It's also essential to expect change to happen. As a coach and learning facilitator, I come across many executives in organisations, even senior ones who cannot stomach change. Some people did not have a need to make drastic change and have gotten used to minimal change. We know that change is constant. While change can be awkward, change is good in the end. So can we be ready and prepared for change and embrace it when it happens. We learn and grow from a culture of constructive feedback. Feedback is like a gift. It's up to us what we want to do with it.

We can only challenge the status quo and grow when we set our priorities and plan to surpass the barriers we might come across. Remember again: You are the author of your life. Do not be afraid to edit or change the script.

LEADERSHIP AGILITY

Read these statements again and reflect on what they mean to you in the current situation that you are in. Place yourself in context to be able to think through them. I once coached three senior Vice Presidents of a global multi-national. These VPs were a lot like the senior folks that we meet who are still thinking about all these things because they didn't have the opportunity to think about them early on in their lives. The organization has a very agile atmosphere due to its matrix work setup. Senior leaders remain in a particular function, sometimes only for three months before transferring to another project or geography elsewhere. These leaders need to be constantly high on physical and mental agility and of course, leadership agility.

One popular book on leadership agility is "Leadership Agility: Five Levels of Mastery for Anticipating and Initiating Change" by Bill Joiner and Stephen Josephs. This book provides a comprehensive guide to understanding and developing leadership agility by using a framework with five levels of agility, ranging from "Expert" to "Synergist," and offers practical tools and examples to help leaders develop the agility needed to lead in today's fast-paced environment. Leadership agility is what the world calls for right now. How flexible are you? How 'open to change' are you? How open are you to criticism? How resilient are you? How reliable are you? The world has enough people, and the world has enough talent. But do they have the right mindset and the right attitude?

THE VICTIM CREATOR PERSPECTIVE

This brings me to the concept of the victim versus creator mindset. Think of a situation in your daily life that can be frustrating. It can be something to do with a work activity in your organisation, say like an experience with colleagues or with the boss. You are stuck and do not know how to proceed on a work problem, and there is a deadline looming when there are personal matters to deal with, further complicating the situation. When you switch on the news at night, you are greeted with undesirable news. There may be many issues at work: deadlines not met, people procrastinating, some shifting blame to others, others repeating their mistakes, issues like device failure before a deadline, social media opinions, a bad hair day or emotional and mental stresses. There can be people who will be unsympathetic to your struggles.

Or even a traffic jam! Visualise this. Imagine you are going to a crucial meeting, to meet a very important person to have them endorse your application for a job. The person will be available within a very small window according to his secretary. But as you set out to meet him for his signature you find that you are stuck in mid-day traffic. How are you feeling right now? Frustrated? Irritated? High-strung and anxious? Angry? Resentful? Even regretful? You could undergo a whole range of emotions in a very short while your anxiety of missing this opportunity builds up.

But you can't do anything about the traffic jam and by now you are raging about why you did not plan this important drive better. Let us examine this situation. You're not responsible for the traffic jam. You have no control over the traffic jam. You would call and tell the secretary that you will be delayed because of traffic jam. On the other hand, what could you have done? Those of you who are methodical might say how you would not have allowed yourself into this situation in the first place. You could have planned to travel early giving yourself sufficient buffer time for eventualities. You might have checked google maps to find which roads are clogged and which are not. You would look to arrive before the appointed time rather than chancing it too close. When you do so, you also rule out any possible fatigue before the meeting. These are all effective methods. But what is the common denominator in all these activities? What are you actually doing? You are planning to avoid any potential roadblocks. You are not responsible for the traffic jam. You have no control over it. But you can control your actions. You could have a Plan B and a Plan C, doing what's in your control.

The first scenario, when stuck in traffic with impotent rage and frustration represents a victim perspective, blaming people and circumstances for one's challenges. Planning for eventualities on the other hand represents a creator perspective. When you have a creator mindset, you would be thinking, "Okay, I've got to start early. I've got to be there before time. I know it will take one hour but let me give myself a margin of two hours because I can't leave anything to chance. I am responsible for this, and I have to be in control. I'm accountable for the outcome of this particular activity. And therefore, at any cost, I have to be successful.

We took the example of getting stuck in a traffic jam to explain the concept of victim versus creator perspective. Observe the following statements:

Why did this happen to me?

This is so unacceptable to me.

What should the other person do?

Who's to blame for that situation?

Who can I blame for that situation?

Who will compensate me for my suffering?

Why can't somebody do something about this?

Such questions are an example of a victim mindset. These are questions that pop up for those with a victim perspective in any situation. Check out the following set of statements:

What can I learn from it?

What challenges did I face?

What response did I choose?

Is there something I can do now?

Could I have responded more effectively?

Could I have prepared better to mitigate the risk?

These statements are examples of the thought processes of people with a creator mindset. Can you think of someone who always has a creator mindset, no matter the circumstances? You might come up with some. But can they be creators at all times? Nobody can be a creator all the time. We can be faced with victim situations at any time. The crux lies in our response. We can be faced with a victim situation, but our awareness must help us give it a creator response. We make a choice at that point. It is our choice to give a victim response or a creator response. When we respond with a victim mentality, we might regret the choice later. We could look to convert our victim thinking into a creator thinking point of view. This takes practice for some. It is the simple intention of taking breath or a step back, reviewing your choices and making one that gives you and your partner the best outcomes.

Today, after talking to thousands of people about the Victim-Creator perspective, I can certainly become a 'victim' if I'm late for my sessions. So, we should be mindful, and if we are so, we can transition from victim thinking to creator thinking. Granted, it will not be easy, but mindfully making the choice helps. If you are one who misses making that transition, then practicing mindfulness helps reduce the gap between victim triggers and creator action realization. This journey to transition more effectively comes with a lot of mindful practice.

Here are a few statements. Find out what perspective the statement correlates to – victim or creator:

1. I am open to development and change.

2. I like feedback only if it makes me smile.

3. I like to set my priorities, and my team should follow them.

4. I like to adhere to the set practices without asking any questions.

5. I want to achieve my set objectives as easily as possible.

6. I continually benefit from further personal development.

The first two statements are easy. The first statement is from a creator mindset, and the second one is from a victim mindset. The third one is a victim statement. The statement can look deceptive because you are planning when you set priorities. However, the operative victim words here are that the team <u>should</u> follow. You give no scope to the opinion of your team members for any possible reason. The fourth statement, too, is an example of a victim mentality. Now do not confuse this as me saying that you ought not to follow the rules. Again, the keywords here are <u>without asking any questions</u>. This suggests blind obedience. You will be ensnared by problems when the rules do not account for them. Moreover, this statement contradicts the first statement that you will be open to development and change.

The next statement can seem like a normal one, however it is a possible product of victim thinking. One can argue that it is also a creator statement. After all, one is achieving one's priorities by looking for easier solutions and there could be innovative thinking involved. But the statement also indicates that one wants to achieve one's goals by taking the easy way out. You have made your mind up to take the easiest way out without even considering the consequences. Even before setting the objectives, if one is trying to make it easy, that is a victim state of mind. The final statement is clear that it is an expression of a creator mindset.

Continually trying to benefit from further personal development can be challenging if people tend to discount the baggage they carry. If people have been working in an organization for a very long time and quite set in certain ways of working, any change can be awkward and uncomfortable.

So, in a moment of reflection, what would you like to do for yourself such that you can face victim situations with better ease and transitional comfort? What can you do to become more of a creator?

SELF-LOVE

Learn to love yourself. One person had given me this analogy which was a sublime way of highlighting the importance of self-love. When you travel in airplanes, you will have an instructional and demonstrative talk about emergencies. One of these is about the deployment of oxygen masks. The crew go to great lengths to tell you that you should first fix your own mask before assisting others. A great metaphor for self-love. Love yourself too. Life makes us challenge ourselves to push ourselves so aggressively and achieve much that we can be too hard on ourselves and before we know it this could be hurting us more than it energises us. Hence before you can appreciate other people, learn to love and appreciate yourself first.

Self-love is not the same as being selfish. Self-love is the cultivation of compassion and not self-centredness. You truly only understand and not judge others when you extend that same courtesy to yourself. Because if we deny ourselves, we are escaping from ourselves. How can we give something as beautiful as love when we have never experienced it from ourselves?

Believe in yourself and discover yourself because the power is within you. If you want things to happen, you have to take a call to action. People may or may not support everything we do, but as long as we know we are neither hurting nor harming anybody, we can take that call. Self-love is our duty also to make a difference to the world around us. It is our sole purpose. Gandhi said, "to change the world, you have to change yourself." Change starts at home, giving the necessary attention on ourselves.

IKIGAI

Let us now examine the concept of Ikigai. Ikigai is a Japanese term which roughly translates to 'a reason for being'. It is a book written by Francesc Miralles and Hector Garcia called 'Ikigai: The Japanese Secret to a Long and Happy Life'. I will briefly cover this concept here however I highly recommend that you read the book for more details. The concise way to explore this topic is to look at this image.

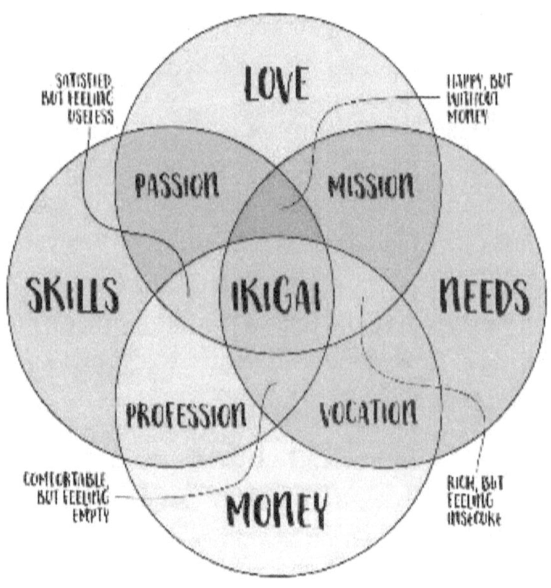

There are four circles here. One circle represents 'what you love doing'. The second circle represents 'what you are good at'. The third circle represents 'what the world needs. The fourth circle represents 'what you can be paid for'. All these circles intersect with each other.

The intersection between what you love and what the world needs is mission. So, therefore, what you love and what the world needs becomes your 'mission'. The intersection between what the world needs and what you can be paid for becomes your 'vocation'. The intersection between what you are good at and what you can be paid for becomes your 'profession'. You might now have a fundamental question: what is the difference between vocation and profession? Let's say the world needs mobile phones, power adaptors, pens and stationery. So, if you can provide that, that is your vocation. It is what the world needs. It's what you can be paid for. However, when you are good at a particular skill set like being a doctor, engineer, lawyer, trainer, consultant, teacher, you can be paid for those services. This becomes your profession. But when you are good at something, and it is also what you love to do, it becomes your passion.

There is also a greater meaning behind these circles. Because in the image, there are also the cases of three circles intersecting and all four circles intersecting. So, when there is an intersection of what you love, what the world needs, and what you can be paid for, it will create excitement in your life. However, it will also generate complacency but with a sense of uncertainty. Why? You are excited because you are doing something that you love. But you may not be as diligent as you can be because you will not be desperate as the world needs it. The sense of uncertainty is born from the fact that you are not good at it. So, you may have some competition who might be better than you.

The next intersection is what the world needs, what you can be paid for and what you're good at. This is where you feel comfortable, but you will feel a sense of emptiness. It is comfortable because you are good at something that the world needs, and you're getting paid for it. But you will experience the feeling of emptiness because it's not necessarily what you love.

The next intersection is what you can be paid for, what you are good at, and what you love to do. You will love this life and be satisfied, but you will also feel useless. You are doing something that you love, and you are also good at it. But the world doesn't necessarily need it. The world here refers to your world – your surroundings, locality, community, society, and so on. So, some of us might have a feeling of emptiness there.

The intersection between what you are good at, what you love, and what the world needs. You could lead a delightful and full life when these three intersect. But as you can see, there is a significant shortcoming. You will not be paid or paid well. For example, someone aspires to be a musician, or a movie star. While it is possible to make it up there, not everyone does. A few do. It could be what you love, and what you are good at, and what the world needs also, but it may not be what you can be paid for enough or paid for at all.

We need to reflect at the spot where all the circles intersect. That intersection is our Ikigai. It combines your mission, your vocation, your profession, and your passion. Our lifelong question possibly is, what is my Ikigai? Life is a journey to discover one's true Ikigai!

Hence to find your Ikigai, ask yourself the following four questions:

What do I love?

What am I good at?

What can I be paid for now or in the future?

What does the world need?

You may not get perfect answers to all these four questions at your current stage. But it's great to start thinking about it. Let me put myself in the Ikigai framework. When I left school and joined college, I too wanted to be an engineer or a doctor like everybody else where I come from. The professions of Lawyers and Chartered Accountants were not particularly well-known. Therefore, everybody took up science for my higher education. And then, like thousands, I wrote my engineering and medical entrance exam. I did not succeed. Now, many decades later, I can say that I am extremely happy that I didn't. I meandered with graduate studies in chemistry and for my post graduate studies took up English and later Personnel Management. I did very well in my studies because I loved it. I graduated from my management course, became an HR trainee. Had I found my Ikigai? Not necessarily so at that point in time. I chose HR because when I heard about it, I thought, "Wow, that might be something I would love to do". But while I was doing my English, my parents were delighted because they thought I would become a professor of literature. My mother tried to convince me to become a teacher. But that was not my cup of tea then. I could not stand in a classroom and talk to a set of people the whole day, every day, for entire years. That was not what I wanted to do. But when I heard about HR and joined this profession, it wasn't because I was enamoured by HR. It was because I loved working with people.

So, I was doing something that I quite loved, I guess. The world needed HR professionals, and I was one. I was also getting paid for my services. Was I good at it? Time will tell. I headed the Human Resources function in my last two corporate jobs. My purview spanned a few countries. So, did I reach my Ikigai? Not yet. But I was on my way because people development was part of my passion right from the beginning. And every time that was an opportunity, I was gearing myself towards people development.

I did not enjoy the other functions of HR as much. I did things like compensation benefits, administration, etc. In the factory, you deal with trade unions, and the whole gamut of industrial relations. But I never enjoyed these duties as much as I enjoyed people development. In fact, as a young HR executive, I once walked up to my CEO after taking my boss's permission. And I said, "I want to train the engineers of this company." I was but 25 years old. But to give his credit, my CEO encouragingly asked me how I would go about it. In those days, we had no PowerPoint, and we had no projectors. We had overhead projectors and transparencies. My CEO approved my plan. That was the start of my training career. 'Ask and thou shall receive.' Story of my life.

But fast-forward many years and over time 70-80% of my work was routine administration, even though I was in a profession that I liked. I realised that in order to find my Ikigai, I needed to move full-time into people development. That is when I gave up my HR career entirely, and I started my second career. Today, eleven years into my second career, I revisit the four questions. Am I doing what I love to do? Yes. Is it what the world needs? Yes, I believe so. Can it be paid for? Yes. Am I good at it? I believe I'm good at it. My clients have told me that I'm good at it. So, am I now living out my passion, mission, vocation, and profession? I believe so.

You can start thinking about your Ikigai right away. You may find that you have it figured it out 50% of the way. You may find the rest immediately or much later. If you have it in sight and look for it in the right places and put your intention out there into the universe, the universe will conspire to make it happen one day (The Power of Intention by Wayne Dwyer). 31 years ago, I put my intention out there, not knowing where I was going.

Today, I've connected my Ikigai with my personal vision. You can too. It's not going to be perfect at the get go. But you are surely going to get there when you go looking for it.

Suggested Reading

Ikigai: The Japanese secret to a long and happy life by Francesc Miralles and Hector Garcia

Quiet - Susan Cain

Mastery - Robert Greene

Deep Purpose - Ranjay Gulati

The Power of Intention - Wayne W. Dyer

Ikigai - Hector Garcia – Miralles

Conversational Intelligence - Judith E. Glaser

The Courage to Be Disliked - Koga & Kishimi

Stories at Work - Indranil Chakraborty

The Art of Strategic Leadership - Steven & Stephanie

All the World is a Stage - Drama and its evidence in the Corporate World by Dr. T.T. Srinath

Epilogue

THE TAPESTRY OF LEADERSHIP

As we conclude this journey through the essential qualities of leadership, it is clear that each chapter represents a vital thread in the rich tapestry of what it means to lead with purpose, authenticity, and impact.

Vision lays the foundation, guiding us towards a future filled with possibility and hope. It is the beacon that illuminates our path, ensuring that every step we take is aligned with our ultimate goals.

Networking reminds us that leadership is not a solitary endeavour. It's about building bridges, fostering connections, and leveraging the collective wisdom of a diverse community through our acquaintances, allies and advocates. The strength of our network reflects the strength of our leadership.

At the heart of effective leadership lie our Values. They are the compass that directs our decisions, the principles that ground us in moments of uncertainty, and the standards by which we measure our success. Values are the core of our integrity and the soul of our influence.

To be a Leader is to embody these principles with conviction and purpose. It's about stepping into the role with confidence, embracing the responsibility that comes with guiding others, and being a source of inspiration and stability in both good times and challenging ones.

Presence is the quality that commands respect and attention. It is the subtle yet powerful force that emanates from within, reflecting our inner strength, authenticity, and ability to connect with others on a deeper level.

But presence alone is not enough; it must be coupled with Listening. True leaders understand the power of listening to connect — not to judge, not to confirm, not to reject - but truly understanding and valuing the perspectives of others. Listening to Connect fosters trust, empathy, and collaboration.

Coaching is where we extend our leadership to others, helping them unlock their potential, grow, and achieve their goals. It's the commitment to nurturing talent and empowering those around us to succeed.

A sense of Belonging is essential in any group or organization. It is the glue that binds teams together, creating a culture of inclusion, respect, and shared purpose. Leaders cultivate belonging by fostering environments where everyone feels valued and heard.

Influencing is the art of leadership in action. It's about guiding, persuading, and inspiring others to embrace change, align with a vision, and commit to a common goal. Influencing with integrity is wielded not through power but through trust, respect, and ultimately win-win outcomes.

Finally, Courage is the trait that underpins all others. It's the courage to stand up for what we believe in, to make difficult decisions, to take risks, and to lead with vulnerability and authenticity. Courage is the fuel that drives us forward, even when the path is uncertain.

As we weave these threads together, we create a leadership tapestry that is not only strong and resilient but also vibrant and full of life. Each thread—each chapter—

is essential, contributing to the whole and enhancing the beauty of the final creation.

In embracing these qualities, we do more than lead; we create a legacy. A legacy of purpose, impact, and meaningful change. As we move forward, let us carry this tapestry with us, always striving to lead in a way that is true to our values, respectful of others, and courageous in the face of challenges. For in doing so, just as great men and women before us, we not only achieve success but also make our lives, and the lives of those we touch, truly sublime.

My upcoming book, *Pretend with Purpose: The Transformation of Faking It,* demystifies 'faking it till you make it' and reveals how adopting a purposeful mindset can lead to genuine transformation. The book uncovers the hidden power of *'being your target profile'* by adopting leadership facets described herein and garnished generously with personal stories, expert insights, and practical strategies, aids you to discover the use of *'being before becoming'* as a tool for growth, confidence, and unlocking your true potential.

Acknowledgements

The list is endless. I am blessed.

Thank you to:

The One who knew me even before I knew Him.

Dad, Jacob Verghis, who I miss every day, to whom this book is dedicated, who's leadership in His ministry was inspirational; for believing in my strengths always and helping me focus on the goal through his life lessons, deep knowledge, unparalleled wisdom and enlightened spirit;

Mom, Mariam (for whom I can still be better), who's indomitable spirit and can-do attitude beats any management guru's teachings – and pushed me to stretch my limits.

Parents-in-law, Abraham and Annamma who's unconditional love gave me constant inspiration.

Annie my life partner and Neha our daughter, for all their love, unstinted support, courage and lively energy that is always on tap when I need it; for being involved from the very beginning of this project, believing in it even when I didn't.

At Notion Press, thanks to the dedicated team for working seamlessly to get the book out in a short timeframe.

Thank you Susan Philip my cousin and celebrated senior editor for your thoughtful vetting of my chapters and being my editorial conscience keeper.

Dean Suresh Ramanathan and colleagues at Great Lakes Institute of Management, Corporate Learning Division whose varied support and distinguished involvement has helped me widen my research and deepen understanding of the concepts described herein.

Thanks to Raam Anand and team for initial writing support, knowledge share and the first interview.

GNR for mentoring me through my career pivot, brewing confidence and showing a path.

Peter Barber former HR Boss for mentoring me in my mid to senior leadership years with great learning that I use and quote even today.

Babu Alexander former HR Boss for mentoring me in my formative HR career years.

Rekha Shetty who gave me the confidence I needed at the start of my HR career 31 years ago.

My classmates Roy Vergis, IBM Consultant Oncologist and Neha Parashar, Executive Coach, Founder of Valyoucoaching.com, who's deep interest in my writings encouraged me from different world views and continue to journey with me.

I can't wait for the next one!

Credits

"Do Women's Networking Events Move the Needle on Equality?" published by Shawn Achor and others in the Harvard Business Review, November 6, 2018.

"The Seven Habits of Highly Effective People" - Stephen Covey Free Press 1989

"Humanizing the Vision: A Journey Through the Landscape of Leadership" by Dr. T.T. Srinath

"The Success Principles: How to Get from Where You Are to Where You Want to Be - Jack Canfield HarperCollins 2005

"The Secret" - Rhonda Byrne, Atria Books, 2006

"You Can Heal Your Life" - Louise L. Hay House 1984

"The Networking Survival Guide: Get the Success You Want By Tapping Into the People Who Can Help You" - Diane Darling, Amacom, 2011

"The Values Factor: The Secret to Creating an Inspired and Fulfilling Life" - Dr. John Demartini Beyond Words Publishing 2010

"The Seven Spiritual Laws of Success: A Practical Guide to the Fulfillment of Your Dreams" Deepak Chopra Amber-Allen Publishing 1994

"The Power of Intention: Learning to Co-Create Your World Your Way" - Wayne Dyer, Hay House, 2004

"La Casa de Papel (Money Heist)" - Álex Pina Antena 3 (Spain), Netflix (International) 2017 for the title song

"Think and Grow Rich" - Napoleon Hill, The Ralston Society 1937

"Presence: Bringing Your Boldest Self to Your Biggest Challenges" - Amy Cuddy, Little, Brown and Company 2015

"Silent Messages: Implicit Communication of Emotions and Attitudes" - Albert Mehrabian Wadsworth Publishing Company 1971

"Charlie Chaplin: A Brief Life" Peter Ackroyd Simon & Schuster 1985

"Take Pride: Why the Deadliest Sin Holds the Secret to Human Success" - Jessica Tracy Penguin Books 2016

"Six Ways to Enhance Your Presence" - Dr. Travis Bradberry Forbes article July 16, 2014

"The Effective Executive: The Definitive Guide to Getting the Right Things Done" Peter F. Drucker Harper Business 1966

"Leadership Secrets of the World's Most Successful CEOs" Al Ritter, AMACOM, 2004

"Secrets of Closing the Sale" Zig Ziglar Quill Driver Books 1984

"The Charisma Myth: How Anyone Can Master the Art and Science of Personal Magnetism" - Olivia Fox Cabane Portfolio 2012

"The Coaching Habit: Say Less, Ask More & Change the Way You Lead Forever" Michael Bungay Stanier Box of Crayons Press 2016

"Conversational Intelligence: How Great Leaders Build Trust and Get Extraordinary Results" - Judith E. Glaser, Bibliomotion 2014

"Conversational Essentials: The Critical Skills for Effective Conversations" David H. Thomas Academic Press Publication 2022

"The GROW Model: A Framework for Coaching" John Whitmore

"Coaching for Performance: GROWing Human Potential and Purpose" John Whitmore Nicholas Brealey Publishing 1992

"Diversity and Inclusion: A Business Case for Diversity and Inclusion in the Workplace" Dr. J. Bernard Hsu Alliant International University 2016

"Diversity, Inc.: The Failed Promise of a Billion-Dollar Business" - Keith Miller HarperCollins 2021

"Inclusion in the Corporate World: A Strategic Imperative for Business Success" - Russell Reynolds Associates

"Rejection Proof: How I Beat Fear and Became Invincible Through 100 Days of Rejection" Jia Jiang Per Capita Publishing 2015

"Influence Without Authority" Allan R. Cohen and David L. Bradford Wiley Publication 2017

Fight Song - Rachel Platten Album: Wildfire Release Date: February 19, 2015 (single release)

"Leadership Agility: Five Levels of Mastery for Anticipating and Initiating Change" Bill Joiner and Stephen Josephs, Jossey-Bass, 2007

"The Power of TED (The Empowerment Dynamic)": 10th Anniversary Edition" David Emerald TED Books Publication Year: 2018 (10th Anniversary Edition)

"Ikigai: The Japanese Secret to a Long and Happy Life" - Francesc Miralles and Héctor García, Penguin Life, 2017

The "Push-Pull Influencing Styles Assessment and Questionnaire" by David A. Schmittlein and Duncan Simester, professors at MIT Sloan School of Management

About the Book

"Money on Meaning" can be interpreted in different ways: prioritizing purpose over wealth, placing value on meaningful experiences, relationships, or work rather than focusing solely on monetary gain.

Is meaning in life more important than the accumulation of wealth, or investing in ventures that have significant meaning that align with our values? It also signifies finding balance between money and meaning or balancing financial success with a meaningful career, ensuring that the pursuit of money does not overshadow the pursuit of personal fulfilment and purpose. It also suggests how meaning is perhaps a more long-term investment in life than money.

Aspiring leaders are looking for meaningful answers to some inspiring questions. What is my personal vision? What should I do to become more goal-oriented? How can I craft a career that is strong and stable? What should I do to become better at networking? How can I leverage my values and influence my stakeholders at work? How can I build a stronger executive presence? What changes can I make for success? What can I do to develop better listening skills? How can I leverage coaching for better performance at work? How can I develop a sense of belonging in my community? How can I build courage for continuous development?

The answers to these questions are unique to the corporate citizen but validate two reasons why people work: Money and Meaning. The Money is vested by the organization. The Meaning is up to the Leader.

About the Author

Suresh Verghis is a dedicated Leadership and Organization Development Coach with over 31 years of experience, specializing in guiding leaders toward lasting behavioural change that drives performance and personal success. He is the Founder of Global Coach Resources and serves as visiting faculty at the Indian Institute of Management Shillong and Great Lakes Institute of Management Chennai.

Previously the Director of Human Resources for major global corporations, Suresh has led international people development initiatives and coached thousands of professionals in Emotional Intelligence, Personal Effectiveness, High-Performance Teams, and Change Leadership.

An ICF Level 3 Master Coach for MCC, Certified Mentor Coach, Conversational Intelligence® Coach, and Systemic Team Coach, Suresh is also an experienced assessor in several psychometric tools. Outside of work, he enjoys long-distance cycling and is a passionate music enthusiast.

Praise for the Book

"Money on Meaning" is a profound exploration of what it truly means to lead. This book goes beyond leadership techniques, guiding readers to reflect on the deeper meaning behind leadership and personal growth. Through insightful chapters and thought-provoking questions, Suresh challenges us to not just lead, but to lead with purpose and meaning. His extensive experience in developing leaders shines through on every page, offering practical wisdom and reflection tools that help readers find clarity on their leadership journey. This is not a read-and-forget book, but a read-and-reflect experience that will inspire you to continuously grow as a leader and find fulfilment in the impact you create.

Neha Parashar - Executive Coach, Founder
Valyoucoaching.com

"My dear friend Suresh Verghis is to be congratulated on this splendid book. Drawing on his own personal and professional life experiences, he has convincingly demonstrated what drives us in life and laid out a roadmap of how we can grow in every sense of the word, throughout our existence."

Dr. Roy Vergis - Clinical Leader at IBM, Advisor in
Digital Health, WHO, Consultant Oncologist